The Celtic Way

The Celtic Way

IAN BRADLEY

DARTON · LONGMAN + TODD

First published in 1993 by
Darton, Longman and Todd Ltd
1 Spencer Court
140–142 Wandsworth High Street
London SW18 4JJ

Reprinted 1993

© 1993 Ian Bradley

ISBN 0–232–52001–1

A catalogue record for this book is available
from the British Library

The drawings are taken from
The Celtic Art Source Book by Courtney
Davis (Blandford Press). Reproduced
with permission.

Phototypeset by Intype, London
Printed and bound in Great Britain
at the University Press, Cambridge

Contents

Preface

No one knows exactly how Christianity first came to the British Isles, though it is a fair bet that it was via the Romans. It was, however, among those least touched by Roman occupation, the Irish, Welsh and Highland Scots, that a particularly deep faith grew up which was to outlast the period of imperial conquest. Through the missionary activity of the Irish saints, and the influence of centres like Iona and Lindisfarne, this distinctively Celtic strain of Christianity had a significant impact both in England and on the Continent, shining a beacon of spiritual and cultural enlightenment through what historians persist in calling the Dark Ages. It has continued to exert an influence on the Christian life of Britain, particularly in its remotest corners and sometimes through unlikely channels.

After centuries of being neglected and largely ignored by both Roman Catholics and Protestants, Celtic Christianity is now very much in vogue again. Books of prayers translated from the original Gaelic or written by contemporary authors in the Celtic style regularly top the religious best-seller lists. Edinburgh University has recently inaugurated both undergraduate and postgraduate courses in Celtic Christian studies and Aberdeen University is about to follow suit. Experts in areas as diverse as pastoral care, spiritual guidance, green theology and missionary outreach are finding much to commend in the doctrines and practices of the early Celtic Church and are holding it up as a model to be followed by contemporary Christians.

Celtic Christianity does seem to speak with almost uncanny relevance to many of the concerns of our present age. It was environment-friendly, embracing positive attitudes to nature and constantly celebrating the goodness of God's creation. It was non-hierarchical and non-sexist, eschewing the rule of diocesan bishops and a rigid parish structure in favour of a loose federation of monastic communities which included married as well as celibate clergy and were often presided over by women. Like the religions of the Australian Aborigines and the native American Indians which are also being rediscovered today, it takes us back to our roots and seems to speak with a primitive innocence and directness which has much appeal in our tired and cynical age.

There is, of course, a great danger of romantic escapism replacing historical scholarship and of our reading into this long distant and legend-encrusted part of our past what we want to find there. Not all was sweetness and light in the world inhabited by our Celtic Christian forebears. They had a strong sense of sin and the need for penitence and often led austerely ascetic lives. Some became almost perpetual pilgrims to avoid the comforts and temptations of a settled existence and sought out wild and lonely places where they could live as hermits. Although they celebrated the beauty of nature, they were also acutely conscious of dark forces and the almost physical presence of evil in the world.

In this book I attempt to tell the story of Celtic Christianity and examine its main themes. I cannot claim to be totally dispassionate since I am an unashamed enthusiast for the subject who believes, as will be clear from the pages that follow, that our Celtic Christian ancestors have much to teach us today. I hope, however, that I have at least avoided the worst excesses of the misty romanticism which has so often descended on modern portrayals of the Celtic landscape.

The Celtic way in the title has a double meaning. I aim to trace the history and progress of the Celtic Christian communities which flourished in Britain between the sixth and eleventh centuries. I also aim to explore the way they lived and thought and to suggest that it is a path Christians might usefully tread today. For me following the Celtic way has involved a journey of spiritual growth and development and encounters with many lively and stimulating fellow travellers, both living and departed. To all of them I offer my grateful thanks for their good company and help along the way.

This book has really grown out of a series of four programmes which I made for the late night BBC Radio 4 series *Seeds of Faith*. I happily record my thanks to Noel Vincent for commissioning them and to Alastair Simmonds, the series producer. Many of those whom I interviewed for these programmes have greatly enhanced my knowledge and understanding of Celtic Christianity and contributed both directly and indirectly to what appears in the pages that follow. In Dublin, Hilary Richardson revealed some of the intricacies of the Book of Kells and shared her unrivalled knowledge of Irish high crosses. I profited greatly from long conversations with two of the leading contemporary scholars of early Irish Church history, Diarmud Ó'Laoghaire and Peter O'Dwyer. Padraigín Clancy gave me a vivid insight into the survival of traditional Irish prayers and blessings among the people of the Aran Islands and spoke enthusiastically about the revival of interest in Celtic spirituality among young people in Ireland. John Ó'Ríordáin infected me with his contagious enthusiasm for all things Celtic, took me to see the high crosses at Monasterboice and drove me across Ireland in the pouring rain. In Galway John O'Donoghue poured out his deep mystical thoughts about the importance of the Celtic spiritual tradition as we sat together drinking Guinness.

In Edinburgh I learned much from two Roman Catholics who teach under the shadow of John Knox's forbidding statue in this most Presbyterian of cities. James Mackey and Noel Dermot O'Donoghue have been instrumental in promoting Celtic Christianity as a proper subject for undergraduate and postgraduate study. Both gave me generously of their time. James Quinn talked with me about the Celtic influences on his work as a hymnwriter, as did John Bell of the Iona Community. On Iona itself I had a fascinating discussion with the Community's present leader, John Harvey, about the Celtic Church's approach to mission and its relevance today. The former joint wardens of the abbey, Philip and Alison Newell, shared their love and knowledge of Celtic art and prayer. I count it as a special blessing that I met Martin Reith shortly before he died so suddenly in February 1992. In his tiny cottage in Scotlandwell near Kinross he talked movingly of what had led him to follow the eremitical life and of his profound indebtedness to the Celtic spiritual tradition.

In Cardiff I had the very special pleasure of hearing

Cynthia Davies reading her translation of modern Welsh religious poems while her husband Saunders Davies interpreted their main themes. Dr Patrick Thomas, surrounded by wooden statues of Welsh saints in the study of his rectory at Brechfa, gave me a valuable thumbnail sketch of the origin and development of the Celtic Church in Wales. In St David's Brendan O'Malley enthused about the Celtic tradition of pilgrimage and at Nevern John Sharkey introduced me to the finest example of the great Welsh high crosses which he has studied and thought about so much. In North Wales, at Capel Curig, I learned from Dr Oliver Davies and Dr Fiona Bowie something of the great tradition of praise poetry as they read from their translations of Medieval Welsh religious verse.

England is not without its Celtic experts and enthusiasts either. Shirley Toulson entertained me at her home in Wells as we talked about her fascinating work on both Christian and pagan religious beliefs among the Celts. Donald Allchin broke off from a silent retreat that he was conducting at Launde Abbey in Leicestershire to share some of his considerable research and perceptive insights into Celtic spirituality. Thanks to the rapidly rising tide, I was able to enjoy little more than an hour in the company of David Adam in his rectory garden on Holy Island before having to travel back to the mainland. In that brief time, however, I discovered much about the early days of the Celtic Church in the north of England. Robert Van de Weyer took me round the Little Gidding Community and made me realise how much the pattern of Celtic monastic life has to offer us today. Mervyn Wilson has kindly allowed me to reproduce the poem which he was inspired to write during a Rural Theology Association conference on the theme of Creation and the Cross.

Perhaps I may be permitted to dedicate this book to all doodlers and dreamers, poets and pilgrims. One of the most important lessons we can learn from Celtic Christianity is surely that such folk are often much more effective witnesses to the Gospel and walk more closely with the Lord than those of us who are ordained ministers and academic theologians.

1

A Procession of Saints and Scholars

Perhaps the strongest and also the most elusive symbol of their faith which our Celtic Christian forebears have left us are those endlessly intertwining and interlacing ribbons and ever-twisting spirals which adorn the faces of their high standing crosses and the pages of their illuminated manuscripts.

Several explanations have been given as to the underlying meaning of the distinctive pattern that we now know as the Celtic knot. Its origins almost certainly go back to pagan times. With its lack of any identifiable beginning or end, the Celtic knot may well have begun as symbolising the endless cycle of existence and have come in Christian times to stand for eternity. It may also have been used as a device to keep away the Devil and ward off evil powers. The Celts believed that the Devil was frustrated by anything that went on for ever and did not have a definite beginning or end. This was one of the reasons why they so venerated springs and rivers with their constantly running water. The clearly defined borders of the knot designs, often made up of interleaved foliage or animals, and the tightly drawn spirals and curves that are so pronounced a feature of manuscript decoration may also have stood for encirclement and protection, the theme of so many Celtic prayers. By drawing in and encompassing the knot, however convoluted and elaborate the pattern within, the Celts felt that they were holding at bay the powers of darkness and chaos and keeping danger without.

There is another theme which I find very powerfully expressed in these most characteristic features of Celtic Christian art. It is the principle of constant movement. The endlessly intertwining ribbons that make up the Celtic knot,

1

like the swirling curves and spirals of the illuminated manuscripts, suggest a world and a faith which is in a state of perpetual motion. This is not the wildly chaotic and rather frenzied activity that so much modern abstract art seems to suggest. It is much more ordered and controlled with an intricate symmetry, a definite pattern and the constant sense of being circumscribed within clearly defined bounds. But the overwhelming sense is one of movement and progress with the lines travelling ever onwards, even if they are constantly doubling back on themselves, ducking under or crossing over each other and ultimately always coming back where they started.

So it was with the men and women who established the Celtic Church. They were perpetually on the move, backwards and forwards across the Irish Sea, the Solway Firth, the Bristol Channel and across the English Channel to Brittany and further afield. Trying to follow in their tracks and piece together the story of Celtic Christianity in Britain is almost as frustrating as trying to unravel a Celtic knot. Legend intertwines with historical fact, promising paths double back on themselves and take you back where you started and characters pop up in the most unlikely places and disappear again just as suddenly. This chapter should really carry a historical health warning. Much of what follows is based on conjecture and folklore rather than hard evidence. A warning of a different kind is also perhaps in order. I have found that attempting to follow the Celtic way leads to the shattering of several cherished illusions. St Patrick, patron saint of Ireland, turns out not to have a drop of Irish blood in him but to have hailed originally from the British mainland, coming to Ireland first as a captive slave and, according to one linguistic expert, being the first person known to have sworn in Welsh. St Columba, whom many Scots treat as a native, was born and grew up in Northern Ireland and came to Iona as an exile from his native land. There is even some doubt as to whether St David actually hailed from the land we now know as Wales.

Part of the difficulty lies in the different names applied to the tribes who inhabited the British Isles and the confusion that this can cause to modern minds. There were at least three separate groupings among the indigenous Celtic population each with their own distinct language. The Irish, who spoke Gaelic and who were known by the Romans somewhat confusingly as *Scotti*, were by the fifth century moving across from their own native land and colonising the west of Scotland. The Picts inhabited the north east, the central Highlands and also the south west of Scotland. The British, also known as *Cymri* and speaking the language that came to be known as Welsh, occupied southern Scotland and the whole of England and Wales.

Broadly speaking, the period which witnessed the flourishing of Celtic Christianity in the British Isles – roughly from 400 to 1000 AD – also saw the dominance of the Irish, or *Scotti*, over modern Scotland (the country which had been called Caledonia by the Romans and Alba by the Celts), the almost total eclipse of the Picts, and the British, or *Cymri*, being pushed westwards into Wales and Devon and Cornwall as the Teutonic tribes of Angles, Saxons and Jutes invaded and occupied most of England. As a result the Gaelic and Welsh languages survived and flourished, the former in both its Irish and Scottish forms, while other Celtic languages like Pictish, Cornish and Breton declined. There are some scholars who feel that Gaelic would, indeed, be a better word than Celtic to apply to the native Christianity of the British Isles. To some extent it is a matter of whether you prefer to follow the Romans, who used the term *Galli* to describe the Celtic peoples collectively, or the Greeks who called them *Keltoi*. Other scholars prefer to talk of British rather than Celtic Christianity, pointing to the fact that Celtic people occupied a large part of the Continent of Europe and not just the group of islands on its western fringes to which the Romans applied the name Britannia.

There is, in fact, much to be said for retaining the familiar word Celtic in connection with the early native Christianity of the British Isles. It reminds us that the saints and scholars of seventh and eighth century Ireland, Scotland and Wales were descendants of a highly civilised and cultured people who had once dominated the whole of western and central Europe but had been eclipsed throughout the Continent mainland first by Roman and later by Germanic occupation.

3

In many ways the magnificent artwork represented by their high standing crosses and illuminated manuscripts and the lyrical beauty of their prayers and hymns represented the final flowering of this great civilisation. Their piety and culture shone out like a lantern from the west into the spiritual and cultural darkness of a continent which for the most part was in the grip of the pagan barbarism of Vandals, Goths and Huns.

The origins of the Celtic race are shrouded in obscurity. They may possibly have first emerged as a distinct linguistic group in the area around the Black Sea about 1000 BC. By 600 BC they had spread from this central European base as far south as the Pyrenees, north to the Rhine, as far west as Ireland and east to what is now Rumania. It is from this period that archaeologists date the La Tène finds in Switzerland, a remarkable collection of artefacts which indicate a highly developed Iron Age culture and represent the last phase of native European material and intellectual development before the very different culture of the Graeco-Roman world spread northwards over the Continent from its Mediterranean base.

There is a theory that the Celts were driven progressively westwards during the five hundred years before the birth of Christ by a combination of climactic and environmental changes which made growing grain in their original central and east European heartlands more difficult. It is not known when they reached the British Isles but they were certainly well established there by the time that the Romans began to invade western Europe around 100 BC. Britain was the last part of the Continent to experience Roman occupation and it was never wholly subjected. The Roman province of Britannia was established in 50 AD and thirty-four years later Agricola won an important battle against a confederate army of Celtic tribes at Mons Graupius, probably between Forfar and Brechin in eastern Scotland. However, the Roman hold on Scotland was always tenuous and the boundary established in 120 by Hadrian's Wall between the Solway and the Tyne estuaries marked the frontier of effective Roman influence although there were periodic sallies further north. North and West Wales and the south-west peninsula of Cornwall and

Devon were little touched by Roman occupation and Ireland remained totally unconquered. It was in these areas that Celtic culture and religion flourished at a time when it was being gradually crushed throughout the rest of Europe by Roman imperialism.

In marked contrast to the centralised and urban nature of Roman society the Celts' lifestyle was rural and strongly tribal. Their lands were divided into small kingdoms loosely ruled by princes. Kingship was regarded as a sacred office and had its own hierarchy with smaller chiefs and princes paying allegiance to a high king. In general terms, however, Celtic society was non-hierarchical and decentralised, being made up of a series of loosely organised and largely autonomous communities bound together by family ties much along the lines of the clan system in the Scottish Highlands. Religious beliefs and spiritual sensibility were highly developed among the Celts. They had a strong sense of the supernatural, the survival of the soul beyond death and the immanence of the gods. Many divinities were worshipped, often in groups of three or triads, and there was a recognised hierarchy of gods and goddesses. Feminine divinities were especially important, chief among them being Bridget who was worshipped as the goddess of creation, fertility and healing. The Celts also had a great sense of the sacredness of places, particularly woods, groves, rivers and springs. A class of priests, known as Druids, were accorded special status and presided over religious ceremonies which were for the most part held outdoors. A high premium was put on learning and on literary and musical culture and special privileges were also extended to the poets, or *filid*, who were guardians of the great oral traditions of ballads and poems.

Christianity probably entered the British Isles through the Romans during the second century AD. It was certainly there by 200 AD. Initially, British Christians lived under fear of persecution. The first known Romano-British martyr, St Alban, is thought to have been put to death in 209 in Verulamium (now the city of St Albans) for giving shelter to a fugitive Christian during the savage persecutions instituted by the Emperor Diocletian. A hundred years later St Aaron and St Julian are said to have been martyred at Caerleon in

Monmouthshire. However, after the Emperor Constantine's conversion in the early fourth century Christianity became not only tolerated but promoted throughout the Roman Empire. There is evidence of some churches being built in Britain from this time but on the whole Christianity does not seem to have taken a deep root during the period of Roman occupation. It appears to have been confined largely to Roman colonists and those Britons who had adopted Roman attitudes and customs and not to have made much impact on the bulk of the indigenous Celtic population. When the Romans left in the early fifth century, much of England seems to have reverted to paganism although some pockets of Christian belief and observance may have survived.

Whether those living in the Celtic fringes of Britain first came into contact with the Christian religion through the Romans or via some independent source is difficult to establish. Tertullian of Carthage, writing around the year 210, refers intriguingly to 'regions of the Britons inaccessible to the Romans but subject to Christ'. This suggestion of an early penetration of Christianity independent of Roman influence is, not surprisingly, strongly supported by Celtic chroniclers. There is, of course, the well-known legend of Joseph of Arimathea and the Holy Grail that would make Glastonbury one of the earliest Christian sites in the world and give the Celtic Church an antiquity comparable to that of Jerusalem and the Christian communities founded by St Paul. The sixth century Welsh bard, Taliesin, who hailed from Strathclyde, maintained that 'Christ the Word was from the beginning our Teacher, and we never lost his teaching. Christianity was in Asia a new thing, but there was never a time when the Druids of Britain held not its doctrines'. This is probably more of a theological than a historical statement, picking up the idea of the pre-existent *Logos* in St John's Gospel of which the Celtic Christians were so fond. He may also have been applying the same kind of argument that Karl Rahner has put forward in our own time with his concept of anonymous Christianity and suggesting that the pre-Christian Celts were unconsciously worshipping the Christ who has always been part of the Trinity but only manifested himself in human form in the first century AD. It is certainly true that the Celts made the transition from pagan to Christian beliefs very smoothly with the new religion being grafted on to the old. There was no persecution to face and no martyr had to die for the faith. In tracing the origins of Celtic Christianity in Britain we are back, indeed, to the symbolism of the Celtic knot where there is no discernible beginning or end of religious belief but rather a continuous sense of the presence of God that simply takes different forms at different times.

Whatever its source, the Christian faith of the Celtic peoples of Ireland, Scotland and Wales was certainly vigorous enough to have a considerable impact well beyond the shores of Britain when the Romans departed at the beginning of the fifth century. As Teutonic tribes overran the rest of Europe, including most of England which experienced its first Saxon invasion in 428, and brought a return to barbarism and paganism, the Celtic lands on the western extremity of the Continent alone retained their culture and faith. They quickly became a haven for Christians fleeing from the Continent in the face of these barbarian hordes and this must have further strengthened their position as strongholds of the faith. How widespread the practice of Christianity actually was among the Irish, Scots and Welsh at this crucial time is unfortunately impossible to estimate. The trouble is that source material during the period of Roman occupation is almost totally non-existent and it is only with the departure of the Romans that we begin to get a picture of Christian missionary activity among the Celtic peoples.

The first Christian Celt that we know of almost exactly coincides with the departure of the Romans from Britain. St Ninian is generally thought to have come from the Strathclyde region somewhere north of Hadrian's Wall. His establishment of a monastery which became known as *Candida Casa* and an episcopal see in what is now Whithorn in Wigtonshire on the extreme south west coast of the Scottish mainland is generally dated to 398 AD, twelve years before the last Roman legion left Britain in a vain effort to stem the tide of Teutonic invasion on the Continent.

Little is known about St Ninian. Although he seems to have come of British stock, he quite possibly received his theological education in Rome. The same may well have been

7

true of several other early Celtic saints, including Patrick, and it underlines an important point about the early Christian community in the British Isles which is sometimes overlooked. There is a tendency in some quarters to view the Celtic Church almost as a rival to the Roman Church which had during the fourth century achieved its primacy in Western Christendom. It is certainly true that there were important differences in outlook, church organisation and liturgical practice between the two Churches but in many matters Celtic and Roman Christianity were fundamentally in step. The Celtic Church used Latin for all its services and generally conformed to Roman usage. It was, however, geographically remote from Rome which led to a certain divergence of attitudes and practices and it also drew influences from other parts of the Christian world.

St Ninian dedicated his foundation at Whithorn to St Martin of Tours. This has been taken as an indication that he may himself have studied at Tours and it certainly points to what was probably a more direct influence than Rome on the early Celtic Church, the Christian community in Gaul. During the centuries of Roman occupation Christianity had established itself earlier and more deep-rootedly in the province of Gaul than in Britain. Indeed, as early as the latter part of the second century the Gallican Church produced one of the leading Fathers of the Latin Church in St Irenaeus who served as Bishop of Lyons from around 178 to 200. His positive theology, which stressed Jesus' role not so much in terms of redeeming sinners as in recapitulating and summing up human evolution, was to find echoes in the teaching of Celtic theologians like Pelagius and John Scotus Erigena. It was also in Gaul that monasticism was introduced to Western Europe and here Whithorn's patron saint, and Ninian's possible mentor, St Martin, played a central role. Born in what is now Hungary, Martin was apparently converted to Christianity while serving in the Roman Army in Gaul. In 360 he founded the first monastery in Western Europe when he established a semi-eremitical community at Liguge. When he was consecrated Bishop of Tours around 370 he established another monastery at Marmoutier.

It may well be that one of the main stimuli to the upsurge

8

of Christianity in the British Isles in the early fifth century was the influx of monks from Gaul fleeing from the persecution which resulted from the collapse of Roman rule and the takeover of power by the Merovingians. A number of monks are known to have travelled from Gaul to Wales and Ireland and they almost certainly brought with them the principles of monasticism pioneered by St Martin. Monks from Tours are said to have established the first monastery in Wales at Llanbelig in Snowdonia. According to some authorities, St Illtyd, one of the major saints of South Wales, who lived from c. 425 to c. 505 and established an important monastic community at Llantwit Major on the Glamorgan coast, was an immigrant from Gaul. There is a suggestion that he may have been ordained by St Germanus, Bishop of Auxerre, who made two visits to Britain in the mid sixth century.

Another important influence on the early native Christian community in the British Isles almost certainly came from the same source that had inspired the monastic movement in the Gallican Church. In choosing to live as a simple hermit and to establish his episcopal see around a monastic community rather than at the apex of a highly organised diocese, St Martin was consciously following the example of the desert fathers of Egypt, Palestine and Syria. The ascetic life of these men who had abandoned the towns and cities of the biblical world to live in solitude and contemplation attracted considerable interest in the West. The life of one of them, St Antony, which was written by St Athanasius round 360 AD and translated into Latin for the benefit of western readers had an enormous impact in Europe during the closing decades of the fourth century.

News of the distinctive principles and practices of the churches in the eastern Mediterranean, including the idea of monasticism, may have reached the British Isles directly and not just via Gaul. The collapse of the Roman Empire in the early fifth century brought about a serious disruption of the overland routes across Europe based on the roads which the Romans had built. Older sea routes were revived, including the one which linked the ports of Constantinople and Alexandria with those of the British Isles via the straits of

Gibraltar and the Bay of Biscay. Excavations at Tintagel in Cornwall show that there was a flourishing trade in wine with the eastern Mediterranean from the late fifth century. Fragments of Egyptian and North African pottery from this period have also been found in Wales, South West Scotland and the west of Ireland. It is a reasonable assumption that these trading links also brought a traffic in religious and cultural ideas.

There are a number of fascinating similarities between the Celtic Christianity which developed in the far west of Europe from the fifth century and the older church communities on the eastern edge of Christendom. Some of the most striking are in the field of art. The exquisitely carved high standing crosses which are found across Ireland and West Wales and on some of the islands off Scotland have no parallels anywhere else in Western Europe. The only comparable work is to be found hundreds of miles to the east in Transcaucasia, or what is now Armenia. In the words of Hilary Richardson, an archaeologist recently retired from University College, Dublin, who has spent much of her life studying Celtic Christian art, 'alone in the Christian world, the extreme west and extreme east preserved an established convention of erecting monuments in stone'.[1] Illustrations in the great Celtic manuscripts like the Book of Kells are strongly reminiscent of icons from the Egyptian, Coptic and Syriac Churches. They have the same artificially stylised way of representing the human body and the same tendency to exaggerate the size of heads. The motif of intertwined serpents is particularly popular in both traditions. Indeed, there are scholars who believe that the design of the Celtic knot was imported from the eastern Mediterranean.

There is even more direct evidence that images and ideas from the Eastern churches had a particular impact on the emerging Christian communities in the British Isles. A carving on a cross at Moone, south west of Dublin, clearly shows two cichlids, mouth breeding fishes peculiar to Egypt, to illustrate the parable of the loaves and the fishes. Several of the Irish high crosses depict both St Antony and St Paul of Thebes, another Egyptian hermit from the fourth century. These two figures also appear in the Stowe Missal, the only surviving liturgical work from the early Irish Church, and are mentioned in a number of early Welsh poems. The sayings of the desert fathers seem to have found their way into the Celtic Church and early Irish and Welsh poems about Jesus and Mary often incorporate material from apocryphal and gnostic gospels current in North Africa. Certain liturgical practices of the Eastern Churches seem to have been taken up in the British Isles in preference to Roman rites. An example is the pronouncing of an episcopal benediction before the communion of the people. There is evidence of a traffic in people as well as ideas. A litany in the Book of Leinster mentions seven monks from Egypt who died while visiting Ireland. Nor was the movement all one way. The British monk, Pelagius, travelled from Rome to North Africa and Palestine in the early fifth century and perhaps found there a more congenial atmosphere in which to work out his affirmative doctrines about the human condition that were to land him in such trouble with the Roman authorities. It is, indeed, quite possible that what has always been regarded as the particularly British heresy of Pelagianism in fact originated in the East and found its most enthusiastic disciples among the Celts of the far west.

Although what was happening both in the eastern Mediterranean and in Gaul undoubtedly played an important part in determining developments within the early Celtic Church in the British Isles, we cannot be certain as to the direct influences behind St Ninian's foundation at Whithorn. What is clear, however, is that *Candida Casa* became an important missionary centre. It played a major role in the evangelisation of Scotland. Bede's assertion in his Ecclesiastical History that Ninian converted both the southern and the northern Picts is supported by the existence of cross slabs in Aberdeenshire and Caithness bearing a distinctive Celtic ringed cross design very similar to that found on archaeological remains at Whithorn. Indeed, both archaeological evidence and local place names suggest that Ninian may have got as far north as Shetland. *Candida Casa* became an important training place for monks and missionaries. One of Ninian's early pupils there, St Serf, went on to be the evangelist of Fife and to establish a monastery at Culross. He, in turn, trained St

11

Kentigern, also known as Mungo, who evangelised much of Strathclyde and established his episcopal see at Glasgow.

Just twenty-five miles or so across the sea from the Ards Peninsula, Ninian's monastery at Whithorn was considerably closer to Ireland than it was to much of mainland Scotland. Not surprisingly, it attracted a number of monks from the north of Ireland and among those who trained there and went on to establish their own monasteries in their homeland were St Finnian of Moville and St Coirpre of Coleraine. Indeed, several of those who were at the forefront of the great flowering of Irish monasticism which took place in the late fourth and early fifth centuries received their training on the British mainland. While those from the north went across to Galloway, those from the south of Ireland made the slightly longer crossing to South Wales to train at one of the monasteries set up as offshoots of St Illtyd's foundation at Llantwit Major. There they rubbed shoulders with early Welsh saints like David, Samson and Gildas. Prominent among this group were St Finnian of Clonard, St Brendan of Clonfert and St Senan of Scattery Island.

Mainland Britain not only gave the Irish their training in monasticism, it also supplied their patron saint. Quite where or when St Patrick was born is uncertain. Among the places which claim him as their son are Kilpatrick near Dumbarton, Birdoswald on Hadrian's Wall, Ravenglass on the West Cumbrian coast, Glastonbury, Anglesey and Caerwent in South Wales. Modern scholars tend to the view that Birdoswald was the likeliest to have been his birthplace. They also lean in favour of a chronology which would put his birth at about 390 AD, his arrival in Ireland as a missionary at around 431 and his death at 461. There are those, however, who would put his dates of birth and death later at around 415 and 490. Either way, St Patrick was certainly not the first Christian missionary in Ireland. Indeed, the year before he went there Pope Celestine I sent out a priest called Palladius as bishop 'to those of the Irish who believe in Christ'. Whatever existed before Patrick's time in the way of organised Christianity was fragmented and rudimentary, however, and he almost certainly fully deserves the honourable place that tradition has given him as the founding father of the Irish Church and one of the foremost Celtic saints.

St Patrick is one of the earliest figures in the Celtic Church who has left us direct documentary evidence about himself. His autobiographical *Confession* reveals a humble and deeply spiritual personality but tells us tantalisingly little about his life. It does, however, indicate that he came of well-to-do Romano-British stock, his father being a deacon in the Roman Church and the owner of a substantial estate. Captured by Irish pirates at the age of sixteen, he spent six years in slavery in North West Ireland looking after cattle. It was during this period that he came to a strong evangelical Christian faith. When he finally escaped he appears to have travelled possibly to Gaul and maybe even to Rome before returning to Britain where he was ordained. In a vision one night he received a call to return to Ireland as a missionary. After being conse-crated as a bishop, he travelled once again to the land he had known as a slave and spent the last thirty years of his life in a peripatetic ministry of fervent evangelism, baptising converts according to the commission that the risen Jesus had given his disciples at the end of St Matthew's Gospel. By the time he died he had established a nationwide church organised in dioceses and with its headquarters at Armagh.

Patrick is generally thought to have organised his church in accordance with the Roman model of parish churches grouped into dioceses presided over by bishops. Yet within a generation of his death the Irish Church was organised on very different lines with monasteries rather than parishes as the key units and abbots often having more power and influ-ence than bishops. There are several theories as to how this monastic takeover came about. One possibility is that St Patrick was in fact less Roman in his ecclesiastical preferences than is often thought and that he himself encouraged the development of monasticism. His *Confession* notes approvingly that 'sons and daughters of the Irish became monks and virgins for Christ' and there is some evidence that he set up a monastery in Armagh before his death. The influence of *Candida Casa* in Whithorn and the early Welsh monastic foun-dations and the continuing influx of monks fleeing from Gaul no doubt also helped to encourage the foundation of monasteries in Ireland. Social factors may also have played a part. A network of largely autonomous monasteries, taking over many of the functions of the schools run by the *filid* or bards, fitted the scattered rural nature of the country much better than a highly centralised system of parishes and dioceses which was designed for urban societies.

Whatever the spur, Irish monasteries developed thick and fast through the sixth and seventh centuries. Among the earliest were Monasterboice, just north of Drogheda, which was founded around 500 by St Buite, a monk who had been trained in Britain, possibly at Whithorn and Clonard which was established around 520 by St Finnian who had been trained in South Wales. Other important early foundations included Derry, established in 521 by St Columba, Clonfert (St Brendan), Lismore (St Carthach), Clonmacnoise (St Ciaran), Bangor (St Comgall) and Kildare (St Brigid).

The pattern of life in these monasteries is described in Chapter 4. It was their remarkable mixture of extreme asceticism, fervent prayer and devotion and highly refined culture and scholarship that has led historians to describe Ireland in the sixth and seventh centuries as the land of saints and scholars. A word of qualification is perhaps needed about the word saint. It was used fairly freely and certainly does not imply that all those to whom it was applied would merit canonisation according to the rigorous criteria later laid down by the Roman Catholic Church. There can be no doubt, however, that the saints of the Celtic Church were for the most part very holy men and women. For all the legends about their miraculous deeds and supernatural powers they also had a great quality of simplicity and this is perhaps one of their most attractive characteristics for us today. When St Brigid, abbess of the great mixed monastery at Kildare, was asked what were the three things most pleasing to God she replied true faith in the Lord with a pure heart, a simple life with piety and generosity with charity. These were all qualities that the Celtic saints exhibited very clearly in their own lives.

The monks and nuns who made up such an important element in the Celtic Church were also great travellers. Pilgrimage, or *peregrinatio* as they called it, was a very important aspect of their faith and they were constantly travelling to and fro across the seas around the British Isles. Several of the most important saints seem to turn up all over the place and it is often difficult to disentangle fact from myth in trying to establish their movements. In many ways St Brigid is the most ubiquitous. Revered in Ireland as a second patron saint to St Patrick, she also appears in Wales as St Ffraid or St Isfryde and in Scotland and the south west of England as St Bride, giving her name to many churches and also to wells and rivers. These latter dedications underline the strong continuity between pagan and Christian religious beliefs among the Celts. In pre-Christian times Bridget had been a very important divinity, the earth goddess of fertility and healing who was also associated with inspiration and poetry. Her name was given to many rivers and springs. When the Celts became Christian they incorporated many elements of this cult into their faith. Worship of the goddess Bridget was transferred into veneration of St Brigid around whom many legends gathered. Thus in Irish tradition she was seen as the first woman priest, having been apparently ordained by a short-sighted bishop, and was credited with performing miracles such as transforming dirty washing up water into beer when visitors came and turning the Lord Mayor of London into a horse when he was rude to her.

More generally, Brigid was venerated as the midwife of Christ, being the person who was looking after the inn in Bethlehem when Mary and Joseph arrived. Many other legends and apparently supernatural happenings surrounded her, often with more of a pagan than a Christian flavour such as the delightful story that when her cloak was wet she hung it up to dry on a moonbeam. We can be fairly certain that there was a prominent figure in the Celtic Church called Brigid who was born around 450 and died around 523 in the mixed monastery which she had founded and over which she presided at Kildare. Whether she travelled as extensively as the stories and dedications from other parts of Celtic Britain suggest, however, let alone the veracity of the miracles attributed to her, is very debatable.

Legend also surrounds the exploits of another great traveller among the early Celtic saints. St Brendan is said to have been born in Kerry around 486 and to have been cared for as a child by St Ita, abbess of a convent at Killeedy in County Limerick. After taking his monastic vows, he founded a monastery at Clonfert in Galway which continued to exist until the sixteenth century. Like many Irish monks of his time Brendan appears to have made several journeys to Iona and around western Scotland and also to have visited South West Britain and Brittany. A famous epic story dating from the ninth century describes a more ambitious voyage which took him and a group of monks across the Atlantic in a coracle to 'a land of promise' which has variously been identified as Greenland, the Azores or even the North American mainland. In some of the accounts Brendan and his companions travelled part of the way on the back of a whale. It is, in fact, quite possible that he did get as far as America as Tim Severin showed when he successfully crossed the Atlantic in a craft similar to that which Brendan would have used.

A Celtic saint whose travels are more surely documented is St Columbanus. Born in Leinster around the year 540, he was apparently advised to take up the religious life by a wise old reverend mother who saw that the local girls were keen on him and felt that it would keep him out of trouble. His mother strongly opposed the idea but he apparently took to it with alacrity and is said to have stepped over her as she tried to bar his way out of the door. He joined the community that St Comgall had founded at Bangor. When he was about 45 he persuaded Comgall to let him go on pilgrimage and led a party of twelve monks to France, no longer the Roman province of Gaul but now ruled by the Merovingians. He founded his first monastery at Annegray in the Vosges region, rebuilding a ruined pagan temple to Diana to form the church. The community grew fast and soon numbered 200 monks, all locally recruited, for whom Columbanus prescribed an austere regime of silence, prayer and fasting, broken only by one meal a day consisting of vegetables, porridge and bread. He set up further monasteries nearby at Luxeuil and Fontaine but fell foul of the secular authorities when he accused the royal family of loose living and in or around the year 610 he and his Irish companions were ordered to be deported home. Still feeling the call of pilgrimage, however, and possibly aided by a providential shipwreck, he managed to divert to northern France and Switzerland and established monasteries at Metz and Bregenz on Lake Constance. Leaving one of his monks, St Gall, to found further communities in Switzerland, Columbanus went on into North Italy. There at Bobbio in 614 he established what was destined to become one of Italy's largest monasteries.

Columbanus was one of many Irish monks who travelled across mainland Europe in the period between 600 and 1000 and brought the light of Celtic Christianity and culture to a continent which was largely in the grip of pagan barbarians. They penetrated as far east as Vienna, Poland and Rumania, as far north as Hamburg and as far south as Taranto in the very south of Italy where St Cathald, a monk from Lismore, became bishop in the late seventh century. The extent of their travels can be deduced both from local church dedications – there are, for example, more than ten around the area of Bobbio which bear the name St Columbano – and from the locations of valuable manuscripts which they brought with them. The Antiphonary of Bangor, possibly the first known liturgical book of the Irish Church which some scholars date from the seventh century, is housed in a library in Milan, having probably been brought from Ireland by monks to nearby Bobbio. Other Irish manuscripts have turned up as far afield as Warsaw.

In the opinion of the late Cardinal Tomás Ó Fiaich, Irish monasticism was the most important religious and cultural influence within what was to become the Carolingian Empire.[2] It may even have had an indirect impact on two of the greatest spiritual giants in the history of Christianity in Europe. St Francis of Assisi is known to have visited the monastery founded by St Columbanus at Bobbio and it is possible that he caught there something of the Celtic love of nature. It is also generally believed that the convent at Erfurt where the young Martin Luther wrestled with the theological questions that would lead him to start the Protestant Reformation was an Irish foundation. It is not altogether fanciful to suggest that the legacy of Celtic fervour and faith there may have been one of the influences which brought about his dramatic break with Rome which was to have such profound consequences for the development of the Church throughout Europe.

Less spectacular than their travels far into Europe, but no less hazardous when boats were made by tying a few hides together, were the constant journeyings of monks and pilgrims across the Irish Sea, the Solway Firth, the Bristol Channel and over the English Channel to Brittany. There was a particularly brisk traffic between Scotland and Ireland and Wales. Several of the early Welsh saints came from Strathclyde – indeed it was in this region that the Cymric or Welsh language is thought to have originated. Among them were St Gildas and St Deiniol who established monasteries in Anglesey and in Bangor, North Wales. There are some scholars who maintain that St David, the patron saint of Wales, may originally have come from South West Ireland although it is more usually thought that he was born in Cardigan. There is no doubt, however, that the monastery which he founded at Mynyw, or Menevia, in what is now known as St David's in Pembrokeshire, attracted a large number of Irish monks and that he had some influence on monastic developments in Ireland. Very little is known about St David although he acquired the nickname *Aquaticus*, or waterman, possibly because of his teetotalism but more likely because he was wont to stand in the sea chanting the psalms and apparently oblivious of the incoming tide. St Cuthbert is said to have engaged in the same practice in the waters off Lindisfarne.

Another sea route much travelled by the Celtic saints was that between South Wales and Brittany, often passing via Cornwall and Devon. Monks seem to have played a key part in the British colonisation of Brittany in the early sixth century, possibly fleeing from the unwelcome encroachments of the Anglo-Saxon invaders as they gradually pushed westwards across southern England. St Samson, born in South Wales around 490, and educated and ordained at St Illtyd's monastery at Llantwit Major, spent several years in another early Welsh community established on Caldey Island and then lived as a hermit on the banks of the Severn. After episcopal consecration he crossed the Bristol Channel with a group of monks and spent some time evangelising central Cornwall before going on to Brittany where he established both a monastery and his episcopal see at Doll. From his base there he also seems to have undertaken missionary work in the Channel Islands and the Isles of Scilly. St Gildas, another pupil of St Illtyd and the principal chronicler of the Celtic Church in Wales, also spent the latter part of his life in Brittany where he founded a monastery in Rhuys after earlier travels which had taken him to Ireland and to an island in the Bristol Channel (possibly Flatholm) where he lived for a time in solitude.

Perhaps the most famous of all the journeys undertaken by a Celtic saint, and the most far-reaching in its consequences, was also one of the shortest. When St Columba, or Columcille as he is still more widely known in his native Ireland, set off from the coast of Derry with twelve companions in 563 he does not appear to have had any clear idea of his destination. As with so many Irish monks, his journey seems to have been inspired less by missionary zeal and more by a sense of penance and a desire to exile himself from his homeland. Maybe the 42-year-old chieftain's son who had already founded a monastery at Derry and established thirty other churches around northern Ireland had simply succumbed to the perennial Celtic *wanderlust* and felt like a new challenge and a change of surroundings. Whatever the reasons for it, the voyage that took him to the tiny island of Iona was one of the most important episodes in the early history of Christianity in the British Isles.

Iona was to become one of the greatest missionary centres of the Celtic Church and also one of its most important seats of culture and learning. The monastery which Columba and his companions built on the site of an old Druid temple on the island's north east shore rapidly grew to house about 150 monks. From this remote foundation, which as modern pilgrims can testify is difficult to reach from the mainland and can be cut off completely for days at a time when the weather is bad, came the missionaries who effectively evangelised most of Scotland and northern England. Columba's arrival on Iona coincided with the high point of the Irish settlement of western Scotland, to which the new colonists gave the name of their homeland, Dalriada. Although the Picts still nominally controlled the whole area and Columba was obliged to journey to Inverness and obtain permission from Brude, the Pictish king, to establish his monastery on Iona, the Irish were soon to become the effective masters of the Scottish Highlands and islands. Columba himself travelled extensively throughout Dalriada. The coast of Argyll and the islands of the Inner Hebrides are littered with caves where he is reputed to have stayed or sheltered and more than thirty churches have ancient dedications to him.

It is easy to be starry-eyed and romantic about the missionary methods of the Celtic Church and to think just in terms of holy men going out from places like Iona in their simple tunics and cowls, carrying no possessions apart from a pilgrim's staff, a leather water bottle and a Gospel book housed in a leather satchel slung across the shoulder. Contemporary hagiography encourages a picture of these monks going 'native' and living rough in caves and other primitive shelters and finding their food from the fruits of the forest. There is certainly an element of truth in this kind of picture but there was also a rather different side to the missionary work of monks like Columba. They adapted their methods to the social and cultural mores of the people whom they were seeking to convert. Realising the power of tribal loyalty, they sought first to convert kings and princes and were not above involving themselves in political and dynastic power games. In a sense they very effectively 'worked the system'.

Celtic Christianity spread so rapidly through the British Isles partly because its evangelists tailored it so well to the norms and needs of a rural and tribal society. In the rather inelegant jargon favoured by academics it was a particularly good example of religious inculturation with the church adapting itself to the culture in which it was operating. In part this was quite natural and unconscious – the evangelists were themselves Celts with the same pagan and tribal background of those they were seeking to convert – but there was also some more deliberate calculation. St Columba himself seems to have played the role of tribal chieftain and political diplomat as well as that of pious monk and was not above some ecclesiastical empire building. He staked out his own territory very clearly, not allowing the monks of Whithorn to establish a community on the Western Isles, and was careful to keep in with kings and princes who could forward his evangelistic endeavours.

Royal patronage was extremely important for the missionaries of the Celtic Church. Indeed it was the key that unlocked England to them. When his father was ousted from the throne in 617, a Northumbrian prince called Oswald was given sanctuary by Irish monks and spent some of his period of exile on Iona where he became a Christian and was baptised. This hospitality paid off when he managed to wrest back the kingdom of Northumbria in 632. One of his first actions on gaining the throne was to invite the abbot of Iona to send a missionary down to convert his people. The choice fell on Aidan who, perhaps seeking to emulate the atmosphere of his remote island home, chose to establish his missionary base on the tiny island of Lindisfarne off the north Northumbrian coast.

Aidan was by all accounts a saintly figure. Given a fine horse out of the royal stables by King Oswald, he gave it away to the first poor family that he met and preferred to carry out his missionary journeys on foot so that he was closer to the people. The monastery which he established at Lindisfarne was to prove almost as important a missionary centre as its mother house at Iona. From it monks penetrated far down into the areas of England held by the pagan Angles and Saxons, or Sassenachs as they were known to the Celts. St Chad Christianised much of the Midland kingdom of Mercia, establishing his episcopal see at Lichfield, where he died in 672. His brother, Cedd, travelled even further south, working among the East Saxons in what is now Essex and establishing monasteries at Tilbury and Bradwell-on-Sea. Daughter houses of Lindisfarne were also established in northern England at Lastingham and Whitby, where the Abbess Hilda presided over a mixed community of monks and nuns, and at Melrose in the Scottish borders where St Cuthbert was trained.

Other parts of England were evangelised directly from Ireland. The prime mover in the conversion of East Anglia was St Fursey who came to England with his two brothers around 633 and stayed for twelve years, establishing a monastery at Burgh Castle, near Yarmouth, before moving on to

France. One of his companions, Dicul, was among the first to evangelise the South Saxons and founded a monastery at Bosham near Chichester. Irish monks may also have been the first to bring Christianity to Wessex. The founder of the monastery at Malmesbury was an Irish monk, Maeldúbh. One of his pupils, Aldhelm, was Abbot of Malmesbury from 675 to 705 and the first Bishop of Sherborne.

These Celtic missionaries were not alone in trying to bring Christianity to the pagan English in the centuries following the departure of the Romans and the arrival of new occupiers from the Continent. Another missionary effort more directly controlled and inspired by Rome had its base at the other end of the country from Lindisfarne in the Jutish kingdom of Kent. In 596 Pope Gregory I sent a band of forty monks, led by St Augustine, to preach the Gospel in England. They arrived in Kent in 597 and were well received by the local king, Ethelbert, who himself became a Christian. Augustine went to Arles to be consecrated Archbishop of the English and established his see at Canterbury. Shortly before his death in 605 he founded two more episcopal sees, at Rochester and London, but he was not successful in his efforts to extend his authority over the Celtic Christians of Wales and South West England. A second group of missionaries were sent out from Rome in 601. Among them was Paulinus who became chaplain to Ethelburga, a Kentish princess who married King Edwin of Northumbria. He went north with her and carried out extensive evangelistic work which was rewarded when Pope Honorius recognised him as Archbishop of York in 632. However, when Edwin was killed by one of his rivals Paulinus lost his royal patron and was forced to return south where he became Bishop of Rochester. Roman missionaries were also active in East Anglia where St Felix established an episcopal see at Dunwich.

Although they undoubtedly had success in Kent and to some extent also in Essex and East Anglia, the missionaries sent from Rome made little impact on the rest of England. This was partly because they did not manage to achieve very good relations with the existing Celtic Christian communities. The British bishops already consecrated in Wessex, Wales, Mercia and Northumbria refused to accept the primacy of

Canterbury while those in Wales would not join with Augustine in his mission to the Anglo-Saxons. For their part those brought up in Roman ways were somewhat dubious about the validity of the orders of the British bishops who were generally consecrated by just one episcopal colleague rather than the three or more demanded by Rome. In several areas the Roman Church was stricter than the Celtic. There is some evidence, for example, that if there were not actually women priests in the Celtic Church then there were at least what would now be called female eucharistic ministers who distributed the chalice. This practice was frowned on by the Roman Church as was the apparently fairly widespread incidence among the Celts of married clergy. The two Churches also differed in other more technical ways, such as the date on which they celebrated Easter and the style of tonsure favoured by their monks. In keeping with their desire to maintain continuity with pre-Christian customs, Celtic monks followed the example of the Druids and shaved off the hair from the front of their heads while letting it grow long at the back. Roman monks preferred a circular bald pate.

The tensions between Celtic and Roman missionaries which surfaced in England during the seventh century almost certainly had an element of simple territorial rivalry. But there was also a more fundamental incompatibility between the outlook of the two Christian traditions which they represented. It is over-simplistic to portray the Celts as the more spiritual, with gentle wandering saints and scholars producing beautiful poems and illuminated manuscripts while the more prosaic and bureaucratically-minded Romans concentrated on regulations and the details of ecclesiastical administration. There were plenty of saintly figures in the Roman Church and the Celts certainly did not have a monopoly of spirituality and culture. There was however an important difference in the way that the two groups regarded the Church, reflecting both their distinctive racial temperaments and their very dissimilar social backgrounds. Belonging to a scattered rural world and with a long tradition of migration, the Celts naturally thought of the Church in terms of loosely structured monastic communities. They saw bishops and priests much more as wandering evangelists than as settled ministers exercising pastoral and administrative functions within a fixed area. Those brought up in the more urbanised and settled world of Roman society were much more inclined to stress organisation and stability and to think in terms of the Church as an administrative body made up of parishes and dioceses.

The debate between Celtic and Roman Christians in England came to a head at the famous synod held in Whitby in 664. Once again royal patronage played a key part in this important episode in the early history of Christianity in the British Isles. Oswald had been succeeded as King of Northumbria by Oswin who continued to support the Celtic missionaries working from Lindisfarne and elsewhere. However, he married a princess from Kent who had been brought up in Roman ways. This led to an unsatisfactory divergence in the religious observance of the Court, most noticeable when the king was celebrating Easter one day and the queen a week later. Keen to introduce an element of uniformity and harmony into the Christian life of his court and kingdom, Oswin summoned representatives of both the Celtic and Roman Christian communities to the monastery at Whitby to debate the disputed issues between them and decide which should prevail. The Celts were led by Colman, Bishop of Lindisfarne, and the Romans by Wilfrid, Bishop of York and a convert to Roman ways who had himself been educated at Lindisfarne but adopted the Benedictine rather than the Celtic rule when he became Abbot of Ripon. Wilfrid got the better of the argument, at least as far as the royal arbiter was concerned, and Oswin concluded the synod by announcing that in future Northumbria would follow Roman usage in matters like the date of Easter and the style of monastic tonsure. Colman retreated back to Ireland.

The Synod of Whitby is often portrayed as marking the ousting of Celtic Christianity in Britain. It is very tempting, and perhaps not wholly inaccurate to see it as an unequal and ultimately tragic struggle between a fragile native tradition of spirituality rooted among the ordinary people and the imperialism and legalism of an alien church establishment. In her powerful book, *The Celtic Alternative*, which is subtitled 'A reminder of the Christianity we lost', Shirley Toulson argues that it was a more significant turning point in British history than the Battle of Hastings. At Whitby, she writes,

> we lost a form of Christianity which, through its druidic roots, was truly linked to the perennial philosophy of humanity . . . The leaders of the Celtic Church followed a religion that was primarily concerned with the relations between people, a religion of an isolated rural landscape, in which to meet a fellow human being is to hail him. At Whitby we traded that for a city-based religion, and in the cities people are amassed in crowds, to be manipulated, no matter how benevolently.[3]

This is almost certainly to overstress both the differences between Celtic and Roman Christianity and the historical impact of the Synod of Whitby. As we have seen, several of the founding fathers of the Celtic Church in the British Isles, including quite possibly both St Ninian and St Patrick, may well have been educated in Rome. The missionaries who went out from Iona and Lindisfarne did not set out to establish a separate or national British Church. They saw themselves as part of the one universal Catholic Church. There is a danger in projecting back into this early period the kind of denominational rivalries and distinct identities which have been such a marked feature of Church life since the Reformation. Admittedly, Shirley Toulson is not guilty of this. She is concerned rather with what she takes to be the loss of a whole outlook and perspective on life. But here too she is surely over-exaggerating the influence of one episode in the early history of the Church in Britain. It may be true that the Synod of Whitby did mark the beginning of the end of a distinctive native Celtic Christianity in Britain. But that end took a long time coming – if, indeed, it has ever quite come. The last chapter of this book will trace its survival and continuing legacy in many different churches and communities. More immediately, the Celtic Church continued as a fairly distinct and recognisable entity in several parts of the British Isles for another 500 years after Whitby. If it looked increasingly threatened and beleaguered, this was not so much by Roman ecclesiastical imperialism or the claims of Canterbury to primacy over the Church in Britain but rather by the incursions of the Vikings and ultimately by the activities of the Normans, the last in the long line of invaders and occupiers of these islands and the most determined to impose their own uniform church structure.

Not surprisingly, it was in England that the retreat of Celtic Christianity in favour of a more organised Roman system of ecclesiastical administration was most marked. Yet even here the old ways took a long time to disappear. Cuthbert, Bishop of Lindisfarne from 684 to 687, accepted Roman usage in matters like the dating of Easter but was still very much a Celtic monk at heart. A tireless missionary throughout Northumbria and the Scottish borders, he periodically felt the call to solitude and regularly withdrew for long periods to his cell on the tiny island of Farne off Holy Island. Lindisfarne continued very much as an Irish style monastery throughout the eighth and ninth centuries. What destroyed it was not pressure from Rome to conform to a more ordered Benedictine rule but raids by the Vikings which began in 793 and continued with such ferocity that it had finally to be abandoned in 883. The monks departed taking with them the relics of Cuthbert on a long pilgrimage that finally ended in Durham.

The process whereby the Archbishops of Canterbury and York established their authority over churches throughout the whole of England was very slow and gradual. That Celtic influences were still strong in the south in the early ninth century is clear from a decree promulgated at the Council of Chelsea in 816 that no one of the race of Scots (i.e. Irish) should administer baptism or Holy Communion in an English church 'since it is uncertain by whom they have been ordained or whether they have been ordained at all'. In the far north and the south west it took much longer to establish a unified English Church in place of the old Celtic Christian communities. It was not until 926 that King Athelstan established an English diocese of Cornwall, signalling the final victory of the Saxons over the Celtic Church there. Indeed, only with the coming of the Normans in the eleventh century were the last traces of Celtic practice eliminated. The key figure in establishing a centralised and hierarchical structure for the Church throughout the country, based in dioceses and par-

ishes and with monasteries relegated in status and conforming
to Continental rather than Celtic rules was Lanfranc, Archbishop of Canterbury from 1070 to 1089. An Italian by birth,
he enthusiastically accepted the primacy of the see of Rome
and in turn asserted his own primacy over not just York but
also Armagh and St Andrews. Alongside this claim to be
Primate of all Britain, he pursued a rigorous reform of ecclesiastical discipline and organisation. Clerical marriage was out-
lawed and celibacy enforced among monks and priests. Bishops, installed in magnificent palaces and involved in civil as
well as ecclesiastical administration, effectively became feudal
barons and the Church was enmeshed much more in the
apparatus of the state. With its massive stone cathedrals built
to last for centuries the Norman Church had a much more
settled and established feel than the essentially provisional
Celtic Christian communities with their wattle and daub huts
for worship, ever-itinerant monks and bishops who regularly
retreated to hermits' cells.

Christians in Scotland also took several centuries to give up
their autonomy and accept the authority of Rome as mediated
through York and Canterbury. The monks at Iona accepted
Roman customs in the latter part of the eighth century and
around the same time the see that Ninian had established in
Galloway became an Anglican diocese subject to York. As in
England, it was Viking raids that finally put paid to the Celtic
Church. In 802 Iona was laid to waste and forty years later
on the orders of King Kenneth MacAlpine St Columba's
remains were removed to Dunkeld. This marked an important
shift in Scottish religious life away from the Irish heartland
of Dalriada to the homeland of the Picts. Many of the monks
from Iona retreated to Ireland, taking with them the Book of
Kells. At the end of the ninth century the centre of ecclesiastical gravity in Scotland shifted even further east to St Andrews
on the Fife coast where a new ecclesiastical establishment
grew up on much more English lines.

As in Northumbria, a mixed royal marriage was instrumental in turning the Scots from Celtic to Roman ways. Malcolm
Canmore, whose rule from 1057 to 1093 effectively united the
Picts and the Scots in a single kingdom, was married to
an Anglo-Saxon princess, Margaret. A devout Christian, she

established the abbey at Dunfermline, introducing the principles of Continental monasticism in place of the freer Celtic approach, and generally tightened up church organisation and liturgy throughout the country. The process of Anglo-Norman ascendancy continued under Malcolm Canmore's youngest son, David, who ruled Scotland from 1124 to 1153, establishing dioceses on the English model at Glasgow and in the Highlands and organising the Church on a parish system. David I also founded monasteries at Kinloss, Newbattle, Holyrood, Melrose and Jedburgh. In 1203 a group of Benedictine monks came to Iona and built the Norman Abbey which stands there today. Although Columba's island was once again home to a monastic community it was very different in appearance and character from the collection of cells and huts which had housed his Irish followers as they rested briefly between their travels and their scholarly labours.

Ireland remained untroubled by external interference longer than England and Scotland. Indeed, it became a haven for monks escaping from the effects of Viking raids on places like Iona and Lindisfarne. Although the Irish Church adopted the Roman system of calculating the date for Easter during the seventh century it maintained most of its other traditions. In the eighth century an important native reform movement, which took the name Culdee from the Irish *Céili Dé* (servants of God), promoted a renewed wave of asceticism and austerity in the monastic communities and inspired a new missionary effort. New monasteries sprung up like the one founded in 774 by Maelruin at Tallaght where new entrants endured a year of purification which involved three forty-day periods on bread and water. For the next three centuries Ireland enjoyed a golden age as the last home of the great Celtic civilisation which had once spread right across Europe. This is the period which saw the erection of the great high crosses with their finely carved faces and the manufacture of intricate metalwork like the Ardagh Chalice and the Tara Brooch. Most of this magnificent artwork was carried out in monasteries. Although Vikings attacked some of the east coast monasteries the Irish Church was able to keep its Celtic monastic structure until the twelfth century when it fell under the twin influence of the Gregorian Renaissance and the Norman ascendancy.

Monasteries were reformed along lines inspired by St Bernard of Clairvaux with more rules and regulations and less contact with the outside world. The Synod of Kells in 1152 gave the Irish Church a diocesan and parish structure bringing it into line with the rest of Britain. Four provinces and thirty-six dioceses were created with the Archbishop of Armagh recognised as primate. The Norman invasion and occupation which began a few years later brought English control over the Irish Church.

The Welsh put up what was in many ways the most spirited fight against English imperialism and the centralising and bureaucratic tendencies of Rome. They held out against the Roman system of dating Easter until late in the eighth century. Down to 1066 the old Celtic institutions survived virtually intact with influence continuing to lie with abbots, and bishops having no territorial or diocesan powers. Anglo-Norman bishoprics were established at Bangor in 1092 and St Asaph in 1143 but there were long periods of vacancy and a lack of episcopal control and authority. In the south the native bishops in Dyfed and Glamorgan continued to resist Norman infiltration and tried to assert their independence of Canterbury. Ultimately, however, they were forced to concede defeat and accept the imposition of a centralised diocesan structure by the Norman dynasty which ruled England and Wales. The modern diocese of St David's was created during the reign of Henry I and the diocese of Llandaff in the early twelfth century. As in Ireland and Scotland Norman influence also showed itself with the foundation of Cistercian abbeys organised along lines laid down by Bernard of Clairvaux and very different from the old Celtic monastic communities.

I have tended in this chapter to use the phrase 'Celtic Christian communities' as much, if not more, than 'the Celtic Church' because in many ways it gives a better picture of the native religious life that existed in the British Isles during the period between the departure of the Romans and the coming of the Normans. To speak of a Celtic Church suggests a degree of organisation and institutionalisation which was not there. Celtic Christianity was much more of a loose confederation of virtually autonomous communities. Maybe, indeed, it was not even that but rather a shifting pattern of essentially provisional attitudes, images and structures which wove their way around one another and around the culture and society of which they were so much a part in the manner of the interlacing ribbons in the Celtic knot.

Celtic Christianity was a faith hammered out at the margins. The Celts lived on the margins of Britain, on the margins of Europe and on the margins of Christendom. They lived close to nature, close to the elements, close to God and close to homelessness, poverty and starvation. They were under constant threat, from invasion by Vikings and other Germanic tribes, from Anglo-Saxon, Norman and Roman imperialism, from all sorts of forces that were bigger and more powerful than they were. Nor was it just their land and their livelihoods that were threatened but their language, their culture, their institutions and their beliefs. It has been said that there are two kinds of people in history – those who do things to others and those who have things done to them. The Celts as a race indisputably belong to the second category. Their story is one of oppression, suffering and progressive marginalisation – the way that was trodden by Jesus in his time on earth. But it is a story, too, of remarkable hope, imagination, wholeness and simplicity, qualities that we are beginning to discern our own need of in a society that for all its outward sophistication and success is perhaps just as threatened and suffers just as much.

The great upsurge of interest in Celtic Christianity in recent years can be compared to the re-evaluation of the religious beliefs of other peoples who have lived on the margins like the Australian Aboriginees and the native Indians of North America. It reflects a realisation that what is primitive and simple can also be profound and highly original. It expresses also a deeply Christian view that it is among the voices of the most marginalised and oppressed that we may find the greatest wisdom. If our Celtic Christian forebears appear to us now as a slightly anarchic procession of saints and scholars who were ultimately eclipsed by those who were more powerful and more organised, then that is one very good reason why we should listen to what they were saying. As I hope to make clear in the pages that follow it is far from being the only reason why the Celtic way is worth pursuing today.

2

Presence and Protection

Different Christian communities throughout history have each made their distinctive and enduring contribution to the ongoing life of the Church universal. Medieval Catholicism embedded the principles of canon law and philosophical theology. The churches of the Reformation brought a greater concentration on Scripture and the experience of faith. Methodism has contributed its great hymns of enthusiasm and its social Gospel. The legacy of Celtic Christianity is simpler and more direct. It has left a store of prayers, poems and artefacts that testify to the presence and protection of God.

Almost certainly the best known piece of writing which has passed down to us from the golden age of Celtic Christianity is the hymn or invocation known as St Patrick's Breastplate. Dating probably from the eighth century and written originally in old Irish with a Latin ending, it has been translated many times into English. Most faithful to the metre and language of the original is probably the recent version by Noel Dermot O'Donoghue which begins: 'For my shield this day I call a mighty power, the Holy Trinity!'[1] More familiar, however, is the translation made more than a hundred years ago by Mrs Cecil Frances Alexander which has found its way into nearly every hymnbook, 'I bind unto myself today the strong name of the Trinity'.

The story that St Patrick recited the poem as he faced the chariots and warriors of Laogaire, the pagan high king of Ireland, on the hill of Tara, is almost certainly apocryphal. Even more so is the legend that has given this hymn its other name, 'The Deer's Cry', and which suggests that in order to escape from the hostile forces of the king Patrick and his monks changed themselves into deer. It is, however, possible that Patrick did compose a prayer invoking God's presence and protection against the evil forces – the tradition of such invocations or *lorica* as they were known from the Latin word for breastplate was widespread among Celtic Christians – and that it was passed down through oral tradition and forms the basis of the eighth century poem which bears his name.

Whatever its provenance, St Patrick's Breastplate takes us to the very heart of Celtic Christian belief. It is shot through with a sense of the presence of God and it powerfully invokes his protection against the forces of evil. These two themes of divine presence and protection are, perhaps, the most marked and distinctive features of Celtic Christianity. They are not of course by any means exclusive to this particular branch of the universal Church but they are found nowhere else with quite the same intensity.

In his book, *Paths in Spirituality*, Professor John Macquarrie identifies the key feature of Celtic spirituality as 'an intense sense of presence'. He goes on to observe that 'the Celt was very much a God-intoxicated man whose life was embraced on all sides by the divine Being.'[2] In technical theological language (which I will avoid as much as I can in this book, not least because it was almost entirely alien to the Celts who managed very well without it) the whole stress of Celtic Christianity was on the immanence of God. Subsequently in both the Roman Catholic and the Protestant West we have tended to stress much more God's transcendence – his omnipotence and remoteness from the world. There is now a growing realisation on the part of theologians that there needs to be some correction to this over-transcendent view of God which has in part contributed to the unfortunate divorce between religion and nature and to our ruthless exploitation of the environment. A rediscovery of the central values of Celtic Christianity, together with an appreciation of the more holistic theological tradition of the Eastern Orthodox churches, can help us to find the immanent God who dwells in this world as well as above and beyond it.

There was nothing remotely unorthodox about the Celts' sense of God's presence in their lives and in the world about them. It sprang from a real understanding of the central Christian doctrine of Incarnation with its revelation of Immanuel, the God who is with us, and from a burning faith in the real presence of Jesus not just in the consecrated elements of the communion service but throughout his creation. This is well represented in the verse of St Patrick's Breastplate which is generally sung to a different tune from the rest:

> Christ be with me, Christ within me,
>   Christ behind me, Christ before me,
> Christ beside me, Christ to win me,
>   Christ to comfort and restore me,
> Christ beneath me, Christ above me,
>   Christ in quiet, Christ in danger,
> Christ in hearts of all that love me,
>   Christ in mouth of friend or stranger.

This celebration of the Christ that is within each of us has clear affinities with the Quaker idea of the inner light that shines in every soul. It also brings us back to the intertwining ribbons of the Celtic knot. The Celts felt the presence of Christ almost physically woven around their lives. They were conscious of being encircled by him, upheld by him and encompassed by him. This almost tangible experience of Jesus as a companion next to you, a guest in your house, a physical presence in your life was perhaps the most striking way in which the Celts expressed their overwhelming sense of the divine presence. It also found expression at a less intimate and more cosmic level in a conviction that the presence of God was to be found throughout creation – in the physical elements of earth, rock and water, in plants, trees and animals and in the wayward forces of wind and storm.

To some extent this cosmic sense of God's presence throughout creation represented a Christianisation of the religion of the pagan Celts. Their gods had dwelt within rivers and springs, mountains and woodland groves. The pantheistic animism which inspired the natives of these islands before the coming of Christianity is well brought out in what is traditionally held to be the first poem ever composed in

Ireland. It is attributed to Amergin, a prince who is said to have lived a hundred years before Christ:

> I am the wind which breathes upon the sea,
> I am the wave of the ocean,
> I am the murmur of the billows,
> I am the ox of the seven combats,
> I am the vulture upon the rocks,
> I am a beam of the sun,
> I am the fairest of plants,
> I am the wild boar in valour,
> I am a salmon in the water,
> I am a lake in the plain,
> I am a word of knowledge,
> I am the point of the lance of battle,
> I am the God who created the fire in the head.[3]

On a superficial reading some of the prayers and poems produced by Christian Celts might appear to express a similarly pantheistic view and to encourage worship of the elements. One of the Gaelic poems collected from the Western Islands of Scotland in the late nineteenth century by Alexander Carmichael, for example, seems to come very near to worshipping the sun:

> The eye of the great God,
> The eye of the God of glory,
> The eye of the King of hosts,
> The eye of the King of the living
>
> Pouring upon us
>   At each time and season,
> Pouring upon us
>   Gently and generously.
>
> Glory to thee,
>   Thou glorious sun.
> Glory to thee, thou sun,
>   Face of the God of life.[4]

There is undoubtedly an intermingling of pagan and

Christian themes in this poem. It recalls the Druidic worship of the sun which was a major feature of pre-Christian religious observance among the Celts. What it very clearly displays, however, is an incorporation or baptising of pagan beliefs into Christianity rather than a straightforward acceptance of them at their own value. Some scholars believe that a similar process of incorporation underlies the distinctive ringed shape of the Celtic Cross where the circle symbolising the sun, and possibly also the earth, the objects of pagan worship and standing for creation, is bisected and pierced by the Christian cross of redemption. In this poem, the key line is the last one. The sun is not worshipped as God, but as the face of God and more specifically earlier as his eye.

We are not in the world of pantheism here but in the much more subtle and suggestive realm of panentheism – the sense that God is to be found both within creation and outside it. There is no blurring of the distinction between Creator and created, no worship of nature for its own sake but rather a wonderful sense that the whole cosmos is a theophany – a marvellous revelation of the goodness and wonder and creativity of God. Like Gerard Manley Hopkins, the Celts felt that 'the world is charged with the grandeur of God'. They saw the presence of the Divine in the sun, the moon, the stars and throughout the earth. In the words of Saunders Davies, a Welsh-speaking Anglican priest in Cardiff who has a particular interest in Celtic Christianity, 'for the Celt creation is translucent; it lets through glimpses of the glory of God'.[5]

A similar baptising of pagan sun worship into Christianity can be seen in the long-standing Hebridean tradition that the sun danced on Easter Day in joy of the risen Saviour. Alexander Carmichael found an elderly lady at Drimsdale on South Uist who claimed to have witnessed this phenomenon from the summit of Ben More. She had seen the rising sun change colour through green, purple, red, blood-red, white, intense-white and gold-white and dance up and down 'in exultation at the joyous resurrection of the beloved Saviour of men'. She went on to tell Carmichael that the only things needed to share this experience were to ascend to the top of the highest hill before sunrise 'and believe that God who makes the small blade of grass to grow is the same God who makes the large, massive sun to move'.[6] Once again, there is no blurring here of the distinction between Creator and creation, no pantheistic worship of the elements but rather a sense that God animates and charges all things with his energy and that they reflect and respond to his creative presence and sustaining love.

This is, of course, a very biblical view. The Old Testament speaks again and again of a dynamic two-way relationship between God and his creation in which the trees of the field clap their hands, the mountains skip like rams and the little hills skip like sheep in praise of their creator. The psalms in particular, which were especially dear to the heart of the Celts and figured very prominently in their worship, are full of a sense of God's continuing concern for and abiding presence in all his creatures, both animate and inanimate. Indeed, Robert Grant's well-known paraphrase of Psalm 104 comes very close to the spirit of the poem quoted above when it speaks of a God 'whose robe is the light, whose canopy space'.

In many ways the Celts were doing no more than following this powerful biblical image of the Almighty clothing himself in the wonders and splendours of his creation. They were also making the very simple assertion that 'He's got the whole world in his hands'. For them these hands are not simply encircling and protecting the earth and all that it contains but also quickening, enlivening and inspiring it. Theirs was essentially a dynamic picture of God's active presence in creation which has remarkable similarities both with contemporary process theology and with the picture that modern science has given us of a universe which is open-ended, buzzing with activity and full of possibilities.

This view of the cosmos as being continually charged and animated by the active presence of God is very clearly expressed in the great credal affirmation that St Patrick is said to have made to the daughters of the High King of Tara when they asked where the divine being that he kept talking about had his dwelling:

Our God is the God of all men, the god of heaven and earth, of sea and river, of sun and moon and stars, of the lofty mountains and the lowly valley, the God above heaven, the God in heaven, the God under heaven. He has his dwelling around heaven and earth and sea and all that in them is. He inspires all, he quickens all, he dominates all, he sustains all. He lights the light of the sun; he furnishes the light of light; he has put springs in the dry land and has set stars to minister to the greater lights.[7]

The Celts' intense awareness of the divine presence in all things has been compared to the Buddhist sense of mindfulness. It extended beyond the physical and material realm to embrace also the spirit world. Here again, there was an interweaving of pagan and Christian themes. The pre-Christian Celtic world was one of premonitions, dreams and imaginings where special honour was given to those who had a sixth sense or the second sight. There was a whole realm of hidden presences which could not be reached by ordinary perception and defied normal rational analysis. The Wordsworthian sense of presences experienced on high hills and in lonely places was very familiar to the pagan Celts. They felt the narrowness of the line that divides this world from the next. This intertwining of the natural and the supernatural, the material and the spiritual was carried over when they became Christians. They were, in the words of Alexander Carmichael, 'sympathetic and synthetic, unable and careless to know where the secular began and the religious ended'.[8]

This sense of the thinness of the veil which separates this world from the next produced a strong feeling of closeness and proximity towards the dead. Once again, there was undoubtedly an element here of inheritance from pagan times when the Celts had firmly believed in the survival of the soul and the closeness of ancestors. But it was also firmly rooted in the Christian hope of life beyond death and the doctrine of the communion of saints. The Celtic Christians took St Paul's famous words in Hebrews 12:1, 'Seeing we are compassed about with so great a cloud of witnesses', to be true in a literal sense. They had an almost physical sense of the great company of heaven which surrounded God, embracing not just saints and friends who had passed on but a whole host of angels and other heavenly powers. In the words of Noel O'Donoghue, 'Man was not seen as being alone with other humans and animals with God way up in the sky. When you raised your eyes to heaven you raised them to a great vast host – for God was the Lord of Hosts'.[9]

It is almost impossible for us, living in a world governed by the principles of scientific rationalism and where reductionist biblical scholars have done their best to demythologise Christianity and rob it of its supernatural elements, to imagine a world populated by angels and spirits. The more sophisticated and educated we are, the more difficult it is to recover this aspect of the sense of God's presence which was so marked and so powerful a feature of the faith of our forefathers. It is quite wrong to dismiss it simply as a hangover of pre-Christian beliefs in fairy folk and sprites haunting woods and streams. The Bible speaks clearly of the presence of angels and the reality of the hosts of heaven. In portraying saints like Columba communing with or being surrounded by angels the biographers and historians of the early Celtic Church were doing no more and no less than the Gospel writers had in their accounts of the life of Jesus.

This feature of the Celts' spirituality was strongly reflected in their prayers. In the introduction to the excellent collection of essays that he has edited on Celtic Christianity Professor James Mackey points out: 'The Celtic Christian at prayer was consciously a member of a great company that stretched from the persons of the Trinity through the powerful angelic throngs to the least of the spiritual persons, the risen Saints'.[10] This is perhaps to impose slightly too hierarchical a view of the spirit world on the Celts. They do not seem to have espoused the rigidly hierarchical view of the heavenly host which characterised Medieval Roman Catholicism with its nine choirs ranging from cherubim and seraphim at the top to angels and archangels at the bottom. Rather there is a greater sense of equality, of intimacy and almost even of familiarity in the Celts' invocation of the angels and the saints. They are certainly loved, respected and often invoked in prayer, but it is in terms of their closeness rather than their remoteness. They are regarded very much as friends and companions in this world and addressed almost as one would neighbours or members of the family.

This brings us to another very important aspect of the

Celtic Christians' overwhelming sense of the presence of God in their lives. To quote John Macquarrie again, 'this presence was always mediated through some finite this-worldly reality, so that it would be difficult to imagine a spirituality more down-to-earth than this one . . . Getting up, kindling the fire, going to work, going to bed, as well as birth, marriage, settling in a new house, death, were occasions for recognizing the presence of God.'[11] The great collections of Hebridean and Irish prayers made by Alexander Carmichael and Douglas Hyde last century and almost certainly reflecting a long oral tradition that stretches back to the early days of Celtic Christianity in these islands are full of poems about the menial everyday tasks of life. Nothing is too trivial to be sanctified by prayer and blessing, whether it be dressing for the day's work, milking the cow or damping down the fire at night.

For the Celts, God was to be found, and worshipped, as much in the little everyday tasks of life as in the great cosmic dramas like the dance of the sun at Easter time. St David is said to have told his followers on his deathbed, 'Keep the faith and do the little things that you have heard and see me do'. This sense of the importance of the little things parallels the Celts' identification with the little people, the marginalised and the oppressed. They had found that great gift which George Herbert asks for in his famous poem which begins, 'Teach me my God and King in all things thee to see, and what I do in anything to do it as for thee'. They appreciated the truth of the sentiment so beautifully articulated by John Keble in another well-known hymn, 'the trivial round, the common task, can furnish all I need to ask'. Instinctively too they knew what sociologists and psychologists are increasingly telling us – that ritual and ceremony, investing even the simplest and most commonplace tasks and events with a sense of worth and a measure of transcendence, is vital to the health of both societies and individuals. One of the most important practical lessons that we can learn from the Celts is to reinvest the ordinary and the everyday with a measure of sanctity, to value again the importance of the little things and to find God once more in the trivial round and the common task.

Another striking and vivid way in which this sense of the

presence of the divine in the everyday expressed itself among
the Celtic Christians was in their conviction that while performing the most humdrum tasks they were surrounded by
the angels and other members of the company of heaven.
This comes over very strongly in the poems and invocations
collected by Carmichael in the Hebrides. A song for driving
the cows invokes the protection of Cormac, Brendan and
Maol Duine in marshy and rocky ground and the fellowship
of Mary, Brigid and Michael 'in nibbling, chewing and mun-
ching'. A milking song invites Mary, Bride (Brigid) and Columba to twine their arms around the cow. A fishing blessing
calls on Peter, Ariel, Gabriel, John, Raphael, Paul, Columba
and Mary to still the crest of the waves, surround the boat
and lead it to the fishing banks.

Nowhere perhaps is the near presence of the saints, the
disciples, the angels, the Holy Family and the Trinity and
the whole company of hosts more vividly or more beautifully
invoked than in the rich collection of Celtic poems and songs
associated with the act of kindling the fire in the morning.
One such, collected by Carmichael from a crofter's wife in
North Uist, begins:

> I will kindle my fire this morning
> In presence of the holy angels of heaven,
> In presence of Ariel of the loveliest form,
> In presence of Uriel of the myriad charms[12]

Another, found with small variations throughout the Western Isles and occurring in several forms in Carmichael's collection sees the disciples as being even more close:

> I will raise the hearth-fire
> As Mary would,
> The encirclement of Bride and of Mary
> On the fire, and on the floor,
> And on the threshold all.
>
> Who are they on the bare floor?
> John and Peter and Paul.
> Who are they by my bed?

> The lovely Bride and her Fosterling.
> Who are those watching over my sleep?
> The fair loving Mary and her Lamb.[13]

This poem underlines the sense of intimacy which Celtic Christians felt with the disciples and saints. They were seen as companions in the home or workplace rather than remote figures inhabiting some far-off heavenly sphere. Mary is more often portrayed as the barefooted country girl than as the high queen of heaven and Peter as the fisherman in the next boat than the founder of the Church. This intimacy has a strongly feminine quality reflected, perhaps, in the popular Hebridean saying that 'there is a mother's heart in the heart of God'. As the poem quoted above shows, it also has a quality of homeliness. Indeed, it anticipates in many ways the gentle feminine spirituality of the early fifteenth century English mystic, Dame Julian of Norwich, who constantly speaks of the homeliness and homely loving of Jesus. The same kind of intimate language was often employed by the Celts when they were writing and speaking of Christ and his disciples, as another poem from the *Carmina Gadelica* shows:

> Who are the group near to my helm?
> Peter and Paul and John the Baptist;
> Christ is sitting on my helm,
> Making guidance to the wind from the south.[14]

What is striking here is the portrayal of Jesus not just as someone very human but also very close and accessible. This is a recurrent feature of early Celtic Christian literature. In Irish he was often addressed as *Mac Muire*, Mary's son, in Gaelic as *mu Churidecán*, my little heart. The earliest extant Welsh carol talks of Jesus as 'the big little giant' who is 'strong, mighty and weak'. A ninth century Irish hymn attributed to St Ita begins 'Little Jesus [Jesukin] is nursed by me in my little hermitage'. This stress on the littleness and the frailty of Jesus is a further aspect of the Celts' own experience of being a little people, themselves frail and vulnerable and at the mercy of their more powerful neighbours. Not for them the triumphant imperialistic Christ of the Roman

Church. Their saviour is rather the humble Galilean fisherman who is a constant friend and companion as well as being the redeemer of the cosmos.

Yet though there is a great intimacy and even familiarity in the language with which the Celtic Christians spoke of Jesus in their prayers, there is no casual mateyness or over-familiarity in their approach to the essential mystery of the Godhead. They may have had a sense of intimacy with Jesus and the saints but they maintained too a strong element of restraint and reserve in their prayer. It is significant that in the great body of Gaelic and Irish prayers and poems collected by Carmichael and Hyde there is almost no prayer in the vocative mood, directly asking Jesus for this or that. Rather the mode of prayer is almost always indirect and invocational – as in St Patrick's Breastplate – calling down the blessings and protection of God in the manner of the Old Testament patriarchs and prophets. Carmichael himself noted that while the language that the crofting and fishing folk of the Western Isles used when speaking of God was simple and homely it also showed 'all the awe and deference due to the great Chief whom they wish to approach and attract'.[15]

God the Father was often described, as he is in St Patrick's Breastplate, as the High King of Heaven. This was a natural term to use in a tribal society which was divided into *tuahs* or small kingships with a high king at the top. For the Celts, as for the Israelites before them, kingship carried connotations of gentle and beneficent fatherhood and wise and just rule as well as power and might. Of the many images and attributes which have been applied to God by different cultures over the centuries, the Celtic notion of the High King of Heaven ruling over the whole company of hosts is one of the most dynamic and attractive. It avoids the powerful triumphalism of the Roman image of God as the Emperor trailing clouds of glory, the static passivity of the Greek ideal of the unmoved mover and the cold and remote legalism of the Hebrew view of the stern judge in the sky. To the Celts God was certainly to be approached with awe, reverence and wonder but he was at the same time an essentially human figure who was intimately involved in all his creation and engaged in a dynamic relationship with it.

The interweaving of the themes of intimacy and mystery in the Celtic Christian consciousness of God produced a strong stress on the doctrine of the Trinity. Much contemporary Western Christianity has become at best binitarian, worshipping Father and Son without any real sense of the Holy Spirit, if not almost unitarian. The Celts, like Eastern Orthodox Christians, had a real sense of the three persons within the Godhead and of their relationship with each other without falling into the heresy of tritheism which proclaims the existence of three separate gods. Their pagan past almost certainly helped them to grasp the idea of the Trinity and the mystery of God who is both one in three and three in one. Triads were very important in pre-Christian Celtic religion as they were in many primal cultures. Pagan divinities were often grouped in threes and this must have made it relatively easy to assimilate the Christian doctrine of the Trinity. The extent to which pagan superstition and Christian doctrine were intermingled, and to which the Trinity was regarded as a real living presence, is shown by the ritual which commonly followed childbirth in the Western Isles until the early years of this century. The new-born baby would first be handed across the fire three times, then carried sunwise three times round the fire and finally anointed on the forehead with three drops of water by the midwife as she invoked the name of the Father, the Son and the Spirit and beseeched 'the Holy Three to lave and to bathe the child and to preserve it to themselves'.

Contemporary theologians, led by Jurgen Moltmann, are urging us to recover a strong doctrine of the Trinity and think of it in terms of relationship, mutuality and community. They see a recovery of Trinitarianism as an essential step towards replacing our rather static view of God with a much more dynamic picture of a continuous creator who is constantly reaching out in love. The Celts had such a sense of God and they managed to express it very simply without having recourse to the rather intimidating jargon of Trinitarian theology. When St Patrick was asked by some Irish princesses to explain the notion of three in one and one in three he did not embark on a lengthy disquisition on essences and persons, *hyopstasis* and *homo-ousios*. Rather he stooped down and picked up a shamrock with its three leaves growing on one stem. The Celts saw the Trinity as a family. Indeed, they often extended it to bring in Mary as the mother. For them it showed the love that lay at the very heart of the Godhead and the sanctity of family and community ties. Each social unit, be it family, clan or tribe, was seen as an icon of the Trinity just as the hearthstone in each home was seen as an altar. The intertwining ribbons of the Celtic knot represented in simple and graphic terms the doctrine of *perichoresis* – the mutual interpenetration of Father, Son and Holy Spirit.

Reverence for the Trinity as the supreme expression of the mystery of reciprocal love continued to be a strong feature of belief in the Celtic realms of Britain well beyond the time when the Celtic Church had been largely subsumed by Norman and Roman influences. Possibly the oldest fragment of written Welsh in existence, a scribbling in the margin of a ninth century Latin manuscript, now in the University Library at Cambridge, proclaims, 'It is not too great toil to praise the Trinity'. Saunders Davies has discovered that the theme of the Trinity runs through much Welsh medieval poetry and his wife, Cynthia, has made this beautiful translation of lines from Morgan Llwyd, a seventeenth century Welsh mystic: 'The Trinity abides within us like the ore in the earth, or a man in his house, or a child in the womb, or fire in a furnace, or the sea in a well, or, as the soul is in the eye so is the Trinity in the Godly'.[16] In the Hebrides the prayers of crofters and fishermen continued to reflect a strong sense of the intimate presence of the three persons of the Godhead as in this lovely night prayer from the *Carmina Gadelica*:

> I lie down this night with God,
>> And God will lie down with me;
> I lie down this night with Christ,
>> And Christ will lie down with me;
> I lie down this night with the Spirit,
>> And the Spirit will lie down with me;
> God and Christ and the Spirit
>> Be lying down with me.[17]

As this prayer indicates, the Trinity was not just a very real presence for Celtic Christians but also an almost tangible comforter and protector. Indeed, it was more than this. In St Patrick's Breastplate it is a defensive shield and a suit of armour to be put on in the face of danger and despair.

> I bind unto myself today
>> The strong name of the Trinity
> By invocation of the same
>> The Three in One and One in Three.

If one of the great themes of Celtic Christianity was an overwhelming sense of God's presence then another was a strong conviction of his role as protector. The members of the Trinity and the whole glorious company of angels, archangels, disciples and saints who surrounded them in heaven were seen not simply as companions and friends but as defenders and protectors who could ward off evil forces. Once again, this view, so alien to our over-rational post-Enlightenment minds, was the result of a mingling of pagan and biblical themes. In part, it derived from pre-Christian belief in a world populated by good and evil spirits, a world of spells and incantations where words had the power to curse as well as to bless. But it also had strong foundations in the sense of demonology and the portrayal of a world in the grip of evil forces which is so clearly found in the Bible. The Gospels show Jesus spending much of his ministry exorcising devils and demons from people. Paul speaks in Ephesians 6:12 about us wrestling not against flesh and blood but 'against princi-palities, against powers, against the rulers of the darkness of this world'. In much the same vein Columba often spoke, according to his biographer Adamnan, of demons making war against him and on at least one occasion testified that he had actually seen 'holy angels at war in the air against the adver-sary powers'.[18]

Those of us who lead ordered and comfortable lives and who pride ourselves on our liberal and intellectually respect-able beliefs may find it hard to accept such a picture of the world in which we live. But anyone who has encountered or experienced drug or alcohol addiction, sexual or physical abuse and illnesses such as schizophrenia or depression knows only too well the almost physical reality of dark and chaotic forces, malevolent voices within and a sense of being possessed by something overwhelmingly evil. Whether through stress and illness, addiction and weakness, experimentation induced by boredom and purposelessness, chemical imbalance in the brain or the wickedness of other human beings, an increasing number of people are experiencing the terrifying and frightening world of possession of evil forces which was so marked a feature of life in so-called primitive societies such as those of first century Palestine or sixth and seventh century Britain. With its great sense of God's protective presence, expressed with great clarity and beauty in prayers which have survived to our own times and which are now being made widely available and easily accessible, Celtic Christianity has something special to offer in the way of practical spiritual help for those who feel overwhelmed by darkness and despair.

A very substantial proportion of the prayers, hymns and poems of the Celts that have come down to us are in the form of invocations calling down the help of God and his hosts against enemies and evil powers. This in itself should alert us to the dangerous though very tempting error of romanticising Celtic Christianity and viewing it as an expression of primaeval innocence and gentle spirituality on the part of a settled rural community who lived an idyllic life in a world unaffected by pollution, greed or violence. In reality life for the Celts was all too often nasty, brutish and short, threatened by disease and crop failure and by aggression and invasion from other more bellicose tribes. Theirs was a hard and marginal existence, close to nature with all its unpredictability and wildness as well as its beauty and grandeur. Their destiny was to be subjugated and overwhelmed by more powerful and imperialistic peoples like the Anglo-Saxons and the Normans. It is not surprising that one of the most characteristic strains of Celtic culture is that of deep and haunting melancholy so clearly expressed in the long laments of Gaelic literature and the poignant strains of the *pibroch*. Like the exiled Israelites, whose psalms call again and again on God for defence and protection against powerful enemies and evil forces, they must often have sat down and wept as they contemplated the misfortunes that crowded upon them.

As the Israelites poured out their sorrows and called on the Lord to help them in their psalms so the Celtic Christians developed a range of prayers and rituals to invoke God's protective powers against evil and danger. Many were adapted from pagan charms and incantations. One ritual that clearly has pre-Christian origins is the *caim*. In times of danger, the inhabitants of the Outer Hebrides would draw a circle round themselves and their loved ones. Using the index finger of their right hand, they would point and turn round sun-wise while reciting a prayer such as:

> The Sacred Three
> My fortress be
> Encircling me
> Come and be round
> My hearth and my home[19]

David Adam, the present vicar of Lindisfarne, who has himself composed some beautiful modern encircling prayers, has written of the *caim*:

> This was no magic, it was no attempt to manipulate God. It was a reminder by action that we are always surrounded by God. He is our encompasser, our encircler. It is our wavering that has put us out of tune. This is a tuning in to the fact that 'in Him we live and move and have our being'.[20]

The *lorica* or breastplate prayers, of which the one attributed to St Patrick is just the best known of many, seek in a similar way to surround those who utter them with the protective clothing of God. There is, of course, a clear scriptural warrant for such prayer in St Paul's words in Ephesians 6:10–18, which exhort Christians to 'put on the whole armour of God, that ye may be able to stand against the wiles of the devil'. But as Noel O'Donoghue, who has made an important and valuable study of the breastplate tradition, points out, whereas for Paul the breastplate of righteousness, the shield of faith and the helmet of salvation are pieces of armour that you put on yourself and which represent your own beliefs and virtues under God's grace, in the Celtic tradition the breastplate is made up of the whole host of heaven and it is much more a case of surrounding yourself with the protective power of external forces rather than strengthening your own inner resources.[21]

Just how extensive was the range of powers which the Celts did invoke for protection can be seen from a reading of the full text of St Patrick's Breastplate. First comes the Trinity, followed in the second verse by the life, death and resurrection of Jesus and in the third by the angelic hosts, led by cherubim and seraphim, the faith of the confessors, the word of the apostles, the prayers of the patriarchs and the scrolls of the prophets. The fourth verse invokes the world of the elements, in an almost pagan and pantheistic way, from the virtues of the sun-lit heaven and the flashing of the lightning to the stability of the earth and the deep salt sea. In the fifth verse the author binds to himself the power, wisdom and word of God and then there is the famous verse 'Christ within me' which has already been quoted. In its original full form the poem is also very clear about what it is that this army of forces is being marshalled to protect against: a mixture of external and internal foes, human enemies, natural disasters and pagan practices. Two verses that are very seldom found in the hymnbooks or sung in church are worth quoting to show the extent to which the Celtic mind conceived of both the world and the human personality as being in the grip of evil forces.

> Against the demon snares of sin,
>   The vice that gives temptation force,
> The natural lusts that war within,
>   The hostile men that mar my course;
> Or few or many, far or nigh,
>   In every place and in all hours,
> Against their fierce hostility
>   I bind to me those holy powers.

Against all satan's spells and wiles,
    Against false words of heresy,
Against the knowledge that defiles,
    Against the heart's idolatory,
Against the wizard's evil craft,
    Against the death-wound and the burning,
The choking wave, the poisoned shaft,
    Protect me, Christ, till thy returning.

But it would be wrong to conclude this chapter by giving the devil the last word and suggesting that the Celts were obsessed with the dark and evil side of life. Far from it. As we have seen, they had the imagination and the faith to find God in the ordinary and the commonplace as well as to invoke his aid at times of disruption and abnormality. They also had a great desire to give thanks to God for the many blessings that he bestowed on them. The underlying note of Celtic spirituality is one of hope and joy not sorrow and despair. This is clear from the great number of blessings among the anthologies of prayers collected from the Irish and the Highland Scots. These include blessings for special occasions like baptisms, journeys and death but also joyful prayers overflowing with thankfulness to God and invoking his presence in the mundane everyday tasks of life. Among the prayers collected by Alexander Carmichael were blessings for the house, for taking a bath, for hatching eggs, for clipping sheep and for tending the loom.

The overriding theme of all these blessings, as of Celtic spirituality as a whole, is a sense of God's abiding presence and protection. They are simple, homely and deeply reassuring. As such, they can, I think, be immensely helpful today to those who are in any way troubled, especially to those with troubled minds. In my work as part-time chaplain to a psychiatric hospital I have certainly found the recital both of traditional Celtic prayers and of modern prayers in the Celtic idiom such as those written by David Adam to be much appreciated by patients. I would also venture to suggest, though I have no clinical proof for this assertion, that they may even have therapeutic value in the treatment of schizophrenia, depression and other forms of mental illness.

Consoling and comforting as they undoubtedly are, these prayers of presence and protection are also challenging and do not simply induce an introspective and cocooning sense of complacency. They are the outpourings of hearts which are not just full of thankfulness to God but also burn with love for all creation and they call those who say and hear them to lives of practical charity. Indeed, they bring us back to the motif of the Celtic knot where everything on earth and in heaven is interconnected and interdependent and all is linked ultimately to God. Here, indeed, most graphically illustrated is John Donne's oft-quoted dictum that no man is an island entire of itself. The same point is also made with great force in what was perhaps the commonest of all the prayers passed down by the Celts through oral tradition, the invocation of God's blessing on the daily process of kindling the fire when the smoored peats were brought to life again in the morning. In finding God's presence in everybody and everything, however high and however lowly, Celtic Christianity also found the most fundamental reason for loving and serving others.

> God, kindle Thou in my heart within
> A flame of love to my neighbour,
> To my foe, to my friend, to my kindred all,
> To the brave, to the knave, to the thrall,
> O Son of the loveliest Mary,
> From the lowliest thing that liveth
> To the name that is highest of all.[22]

50

3
The Goodness of Nature

Within the Christian tradition there have been two very different ways of viewing the nature of the work accomplished by Jesus Christ or what in technical theological terms is known as soteriology. One takes as its starting point the biblical story of the fall and the doctrine of original sin and sees Christ's work as being our salvation from sin and its terrible consequences. The other takes a more positive view of the world, and the human condition, seeing it not so much as radically tainted by sin but rather as immature and incomplete, and viewing Christ as the one who perfects creation and lifts it up to God.

Since the time of Augustine at least, Christians in the West have generally leaned towards the first view. Medieval Catholicism dwelt heavily on the fall and its consequences, the Protestant Reformers of the sixteenth century even more so. In the last few decades, however, there has been a strong reaction against the negativity of this sin-centred Christianity. A new creation-centred spirituality has developed which stresses the goodness of both the natural and the human world. The most radical exponent of this new movement has been Matthew Fox, a Dominican scholar based in California, who has argued in his book, *Original Blessing*, that Christians should jettison the whole doctrine of original sin and develop a new theology which celebrates the goodness of creation.

As we saw in the last chapter, our Celtic Christian forebears were well aware of the power of evil and sin in the world. They were not naive innocents and blind optimists who like Dr Pangloss in Voltaire's *Candide* believed that all was for the best in the best of all possible worlds. They did, however, espouse quite unashamedly and unconsciously what would nowadays be called a creation-centred spirituality. The God whom they worshipped was not conceived of primarily as the Lord of history, as in so much later Western theology, but rather as the Lord of Creation, the one who has revealed himself most fully and characteristically in the wonders and splendours of the natural world. This was above all why they wanted to worship him, as this ninth century Irish poem clearly shows:

> Let us adore the Lord,
>> Maker of wondrous works,
> Great bright heaven with its angels,
> The white-waved sea on the earth.[1]

The artwork which the Celts have left us as their most tangible legacy is full of the exuberant celebration of creation. The borders of the illustrations in their illuminated manuscripts are often made up of intertwining patterns of fruit and foliage. Beautifully executed drawings of birds and animals serve as punctuation marks on the pages of script. The distinctive feature of the Celtic Cross is the circle of creation, representing the earth and the sun, which surrounds and encompasses the cross of redemption. In so far as there was a distinctive Celtic theology, it too stressed the essential goodness of nature, including human nature, and saw Jesus Christ as the one who was sent not so much to rescue the world from the consequences of the fall as to complete and perfect it. This view, indeed, came to be expressed in what was for long regarded, and perhaps is still, as the particularly British heresy of Pelagianism. In fact, the unfortunate monk Pelagius who gave his name to this heresy, and the other great theologian of the Celtic Church, John Scotus Erigena, who also ran into trouble with the Roman authorities over his views, were in many ways very orthodox in their beliefs and do not deserve the bad press that they have had over the centuries. Probably their biggest crime was to cross swords with the great Augustine and to dare to challenge his radical doctrine of original sin and total depravity. Now that we are at last seeking to escape from the gloomy shadow that Augustine and the Reformers have cast over Western Christianity for so long, we would do well to let the Celts be our guides to the sunnier climes of creation-centred spirituality.

The Celtic Christian celebration of the goodness of creation sprang from three main roots. The first was biblical. It is impossible to read far in the Old Testament without being struck by the theme of the essential goodness and preciousness of the natural world in the eyes of God and of his enduring concern for all his creatures. Indeed, one needs to go no further than the opening chapter of Genesis to read the recurrent refrain 'and God saw that it was good' applied at the end of every stage of the creation process. Further into the Old Testament, the Psalms, which were so dear to the heart of the Celts and so prominent in their worship, are filled with a sense of the wonders of nature, from the heavens stretched out like a curtain to the cedars of Lebanon where the birds build their nests and the high hills which are a refuge for the mountain goats. The Hebrew prophets talk of a reciprocal relationship between God and his creation, involving even seemingly inanimate objects as in Isaiah's famous passage about the mountains and the hills breaking forth into singing and the trees of the field clapping their hands. This kind of language directly inspired much Celtic poetry and prayer, including the great praise poems which are such a beautiful feature of the Welsh religious tradition. The very earliest known such verse in Welsh, dating from the ninth century, begins with lines that could have come almost straight from Isaiah:

> Almighty Creator, who hast made all things,
> The world cannot express all thy glories,
> Even though the grass and the trees should sing.[2]

The second main influence came from the Celts' pagan inheritance. The native religion of Britain in pre-Christian times was a form of Druid nature mysticism which worshipped rivers, forests and hills as the dwelling places of divinities and sacred spirits. In common with other so-called primitive people living close to nature, like the American Indians and the Australian Aborigines, the pagan Celts had enormous respect for the natural world and took great care not to pollute water supplies or unnecessarily damage trees. They retained this attitude of reverence and respect for nature when they became Christians. The monks and missionaries who converted them were happy to accept this creationist element in the primal pagan faith of the people and to baptise and incorporate it within Christianity. Monasteries were built on the site of sacred Druid groves, springs and wells which had been associated with pagan deities were given saints' names and ceremonies celebrating creation such as well dressing, harvest festivals and the blessing of crops were incorporated into the Church's calendar.

Thirdly, and most directly, Celtic Christians derived their sense of the goodness of creation from living so close to nature and having the time and the temperament to study and contemplate its variety and beauty. They tended to establish their monastic settlements in wild and remote places, having a particular penchant for islands and often retreating to caves and cells for seclusion. It was hardly surprising that they grew to love the cry of sea birds, the barking of seals and even the buzzing of the insects who were sometimes their only companions. A love of nature for its own sake echoes through many of the writings of the Celtic monks, as in this beautiful Irish poem attributed to Abbot Manchin Leith who died in 665 but probably dating from the ninth century:

> I wish, O Son of the living God,
> O ancient, eternal King,
> for a hidden little hut in the wilderness,
> that it may be my dwelling.
>
> An all-grey lithe little lark
> to be by its side,
> a clear pool to wash away sins
> through the grace of the Holy Spirit.
>
> Quite near a beautiful wood
> around it on every side,
> to nurse many-voiced birds,
> hiding it with its shelter.

A southern aspect for warmth,
a little brook across its floor,
a choice land with many gracious gifts
such as be good for every plant.[3]

The early published lives of the Celtic saints give a picture
of men and women who were deeply attached to animals and
birds. Columba taught the monks on Iona to show hospitality
not just to their human visitors but also to the birds which
came to the island. Once, he called one of the brothers and
told him to watch for a crane flying over from Ireland. The
bird was to be carried up from the shore, taken to a house
and fed and looked after for three days. The crane duly
arrived and the brother did as he had been bidden. Columba
commended him, 'God bless you, my son, because you have
tended well our pilgrim guest'.[4] Another lovely story recounts
that Kevin of Glendalough was once engaged in a vigil with
his arms outstretched in the manner of the cross of St Andrew
when a blackbird came and laid a clutch of eggs in the palm
of his outstretched hand. Not wishing to disturb the bird, he
maintained his uncomfortable position for several weeks until
her babies had hatched.

There are many stories of the Celtic saints developing very
close bonds with wild animals in the same way that Our Lord
did during his temptation when, according to Mark's account,
he was cast into the wilderness among the wild beasts and
yet they did not hurt him. During his periods of fasting
and solitude, Columbanus was apparently in the habit of
summoning beasts and birds who would come to him without
delay, sporting and playing 'like little puppies around their
master'. On one occasion twelve wolves came up to him while
he was repeating a psalm and stood peacefully with him
before going away. On another he persuaded a bear to leave
its cave so that he could use it as a hermitage. Bede reports
that as St Cuthbert emerged from the North Sea after one of
his long vigils of prayer in the cold waters off Lindisfarne two
otters followed him onto the sand, prostrating themselves and
licking his feet to warm them before drying him with their
fur. St Serf had a pet robin and a lamb that followed him
about and is said to have raised a dead pig to life. Ciaran

was helped in the task of digging a cemetery at Saighir by a wild boar which set to work with its tusks to clear and level the ground. It stayed on to become his servant, being joined by a badger, a deer and a fox which carried his psalter for him. Mochua, an Irish disciple of Columba, lived as a hermit and his only companions were a cock, a mouse and a fly. Each helped him with his work, the cock crowing at midnight to wake him for mattins, the mouse nibbling his ear to wake him up in time for his first morning office and the fly walking along each line as he read from his psalter and remaining at the place where he finished so that after a rest he could take up chanting the psalms where he had left off.

Perhaps the best known and most moving story of this kind is that in Adamnan's life of Columba which describes the premonition of the saint's impending death on the part of the white horse which carried the milk for the monastery. On what turned out to be the last day of his life, the horse approached the elderly Columba, put its head in his bosom 'and like a human being let tears fall freely on the lap of the saint'.[5] These accounts of the remarkably close relationships which the Celtic saints developed with animals are very similar to the well-known stories that were later to grow up around the figure of St Francis. We have already noted that the Italian saint is known to have visited the monastic community at Bobbio founded by Columbanus. There were several other monasteries founded by Irish monks in the vicinity of Assisi. It could be that the man who is regarded as the patron saint of animals and the founding father of Christian ecology derived his sense of the sacredness and importance to God of his non-human creatures from the Celtic tradition.

It is noticeable how frequently and prominently birds and animals feature in Celtic Christian art. The artist responsible for the page in the Book of Kells which illustrates the birth of Christ, as recorded in Matthew 1:18, managed to cram four human figures, four animals and twelve birds into a lozenge the size of a postage stamp which stands at the intersection of the two Greek letters *Chi* and *Rho* and is thought to represent the incarnate *Logos*. Lower down the same page he drew a cat playing with its kittens, an otter catching a fish, two moths on a lozenge and two mice nibbling at the host. Among the species portrayed on panels of the Irish high crosses are ravens, doves, wrens, frogs, lions, deer, cats, sheep and snakes. Several of the crosses, including the one dedicated to St Martin on Iona, graphically illustrate the Celts' blending of pagan nature religion and Christianity by displaying carvings of birds, animals and plants on one side and scenes from the Bible on the other. Their function as focal points for outdoor worship further underlines the Celts' love of nature and their preference for celebrating God's goodness in the open air rather than in some dark ecclesiastical building constructed to shut out the light and sounds of the outside world. If the greenhouse effect really is going to give us warmer weather in the northern hemisphere, maybe we should think seriously about following our ancestors in this practice and taking more of our own worship out of doors where we can join with the natural world in praising the Lord of creation.

This delight in nature is also a prominent theme of Celtic poetry. There is a lovely early Irish poem which portrays Paradise as a tree laden with green branches bearing the choicest leaves and fruit around which 'glorious flocks of singing birds celebrate their truth'. Another eighth century Irish poem begins:

> Only a fool would fail
> To praise God in his might,
> When the tiny mindless birds
> Praise Him in their flight.[6]

Kuno Meyer, who translated many of these old Irish poems into English in the early years of this century, was of the opinion that 'in nature poetry the Gaelic muse may vie with that of any other nation. Indeed, these poems occupy a unique position in the literature of the world. To seek out and watch and love Nature, in its tiniest phenomena as in its grandest, was given to no people so early and so fully as to the Celt'.[7]

Underlying this love of nature was a deeper sense of the sacredness of the earth itself and its closeness to humankind. This is, of course, once again a very biblical perspective. God reminds Adam in Genesis 3:19 that he is but dust and to dust he shall return. The Hebrew word *Adam* for mankind has the same root as the word for earth, *adama*. A similar point is made in our own language with the word humility which derives from *humus*, the Latin word for soil. To fulfil the Christian calling and walk humbly is to keep ever in mind the close ties that bind us to the earth. The Celts were very conscious of this aspect of humility. In Welsh there is a special word for it, *iselder*, which is perhaps best translated as lowliness, remaining down to earth and not making too much of yourself. It was the same quality that made St Cuthbert disdain the royal gift of a horse to help cover the great distances around his Northumbrian diocese. He preferred to walk because that way he was both closer to the ground and closer to the people. It is there, too, in the simplicity of the lifestyle practised by the Irish hermits like Kevin who, after settling at Glendalough, is said to have eaten only nuts of the wood and plants of the ground, to have had no bed but a pillow of stone and no roof over his head but just the skins of wild beasts to cover him.

The Celts have much to teach us today about our relationship with the rest of creation as well as with our fellow human beings. Quite alien to them was the idea of domination which has crept into our consciousness as a result of a quite erroneous interpretation of God's commission to humankind in Genesis 1:28. They preferred rather to take their text from Christ – 'Inasmuch as ye have done it unto one of the least of these my brethren, ye have done it unto me' – and to apply it to the birds, the animals and the insects, the most vulnerable of God's creatures, as well as to the weakest and least powerful among the human part of creation. This active and burning compassion sprang from their conviction that the natural world just as much as the human is charged with sparks of the divine presence and reflections of the glory of the Cosmic Christ.

> There is no plant in the ground
> But is full of His virtue,
> There is no form in the strand
> But is full of His blessing.

There is no life in the sea,
There is no creature in the river,
There is naught in the firmament,
But proclaims His goodness.

There is no bird on the wing,
There is no star in the sky,
There is nothing beneath the sun,
But proclaims his goodness.[8]

The Celts were prime exponents of what is technically called natural theology, the idea that the existence of God can be confirmed, if not actually proved, through a contemplation of the beauty and order of the natural world. They believed strongly that the earth and all its wonders provide the key not just to establishing the existence of God but also to finding out more about him. As an ancient Irish commentary on Psalm 19 puts it, 'The elements sound and show forth the knowledge of God'. According to a cathechism attributed to St Ninian of Whithorn the fruit of all study is 'to perceive the eternal word of God reflected in every plant and insect, every bird and animal and every man and woman'. St Columbanus was even more emphatic: 'Understand the creation if you would wish to know the Creator . . . For those who wish to know the great deep must first review the natural world.'[9]

Natural theology is being rediscovered in our own age as astronomers and physicists seem to be pointing to something beautiful and mysterious at the furthest extremities of space and at the very heart of matter. They are helping us to regain something of the sense of awe and wonder with which our ancestors looked on the world about them and gazed up at the heavens. A recovery of the Celts' ability to find God's love and glory reflected throughout the natural world is going to be essential if we are to save our planet from environmental destruction. But scarcely less important for us today is a return to that other long neglected theme of Celtic Christianity – a view of human nature not as being radically tainted by sin and evil, intrinsically corrupt and degenerate, but as imprinted with the image of God, full of potential and opportunity, longing for completion and perfection.

As with their overall sense of the goodness of creation, it is possible to detect several influences behind the Celts' positive and affirmative view of human nature. There is a clear carry over from pre-Christian beliefs. The Druids had a high view of human potentiality and free will and believed in the importance of morality and leading a consciously good life. The Bible, and especially the Old Testament, was another influence: the Celts took seriously the statement in Genesis 1:26 that humans were created in the image of God and the affirmation in Psalm 8 that man stands only a little lower than the angels and is crowned with glory and honour.

The influence of Eastern theology may also have been an important factor. It is perhaps no coincidence that Pelagius, the Celtic theologian who supremely articulated a Christian doctrine of the basic goodness of humanity, spent the latter part of his life in Egypt. The Greek fathers of the Eastern Church had a strong sense of human kinship with God and taught that the divine spark which is kindled in every human being at birth is never extinguished by sin. Indeed, they went further and argued that humans are by nature 'open upwards' and destined to share fellowship with God. Human life as a whole and the religious life in particular were seen as a pilgrimage towards this destiny. The third century Egyptian theologian Origen portrayed the gradual ascent of the human soul to God in terms of its restoration to its original state. The fourth century mystic and theologian Gregory of Nyssa took this idea further and wrote eloquently of the soul longing and striving to achieve communion with God. Much stress was laid on Paul's majestic statement in 1 Corinthians 15:28 about the end time when Christ will have completed his work of reconciling and gathering up all of creation so 'that God may be all in all'. This produced a belief in an ultimate and universal salvation in which all things would return to God through Christ. More immediately it also encouraged a doctrine of perfectionism and a belief that it was possible for humans to achieve a state of sinlessness in this world.

This kind of thinking may also have spread to the Celtic Christian communities in the British Isles from a source rather closer to home. Leaders of the Gallican Church held similar views to those of the Eastern fathers about the destiny and potentiality of human nature. Outstanding among them was Irenaeus, Bishop of Lyons in the late second century, who taught that it was the human being's natural destiny to be carried upwards towards God. 'If the Word has been made man', he wrote, 'it is so that men may be made gods'. As far as he was concerned the sending of Jesus to live on earth was not some kind of emergency rescue package that God had to put into operation to save humans from sin but rather a key stage in an ongoing process of recapitulation and gathering everything up. Humanity was not so much fallen and hopelessly flawed by sin but rather immature and striving for completion and perfection.

I suspect that the Celts may also have been led towards an affirmative view of human nature and its destiny through their own experience as a people living on the margins and frequently under threat. The influence of purely external factors on the theology of different societies is a fascinating subject which has received remarkably little attention. Could it be, for instance, that the doctrine of *kenosis*, which speaks of the self-emptying of Christ as he divested himself of all power and status, was so popular among nineteenth century English churchmen because this powerful imperialistic generation realised that their besetting sin was that of pride and arrogance? The Celtic communities suffered from the opposite syndrome, feeling low self-esteem and lack of confidence because of their remote and marginal position and their constant vulnerability to attack and takeover by their more powerful neighbours. It was hardly surprising that in their theology they should take a positive view of the human potential and stress the role of Christ as that of liberator and enabler rather than judge and reprover. The same kind of experience among oppressed and vulnerable groups in our own age has led to the development of liberation theology among the base communities of Latin America and the shanty towns of southern Africa. Here, as in the early Celtic Church, the reality of sin and evil in the world is not denied but it is seen as lying in external forces of oppression and aggression and not centred on the innate depravity of humankind. The stress is not on cutting sinful humanity down to size but rather on liberating and encouraging people to fulfil their potential and achieve their destiny of communion with God.

Many of these themes can be discerned in the work of the first and most famous Celtic theologian, Pelagius. It is unfortunate and almost certainly profoundly unjust that his name should have come down to us as the founder of a heresy which has always been particularly associated with the British Isles. Recent analysis of his thinking suggests that it was, in fact, highly orthodox, following in the tradition established by the early fathers and in keeping with the teaching of the Church in both the East and the West. It seems rather that it was his arch-opponent Augustine who introduced new and alien concepts into Christian theology and who should more accurately be described as heterodox in his views.

We know very little about Pelagius' life. He was born in Britain or Ireland around 350, spent a considerable period in Rome and died around 418 in Egypt or elsewhere in the eastern Mediterranean. Unfortunately the texts of his major theological works, treatises on free will and on nature, have not survived. While in Rome he is said to have been appalled by the prevailing laxity of behaviour among Christians and to have worked to reform moral standards both through his own personal example and by preaching on the evils of accumulating riches and a self-indulgent lifestyle. It may well have been these activities rather than his theology which made the authorities uncomfortable and lay behind his excommunication by Pope Innocent I.

For such an apparently upright and even saintly figure who seems not only to have preached but also to have practised a simple and virtuous life, Pelagius had a remarkable talent for antagonising his contemporaries. St Jerome reportedly described him as 'a most stupid fellow heavy with Scottish [i.e. Irish] porridge'. It was his particular misfortune to fall foul of the most influential theologian in the early Western Church, St Augustine of Hippo. Any analysis of the controversy between the two men is in danger of being rather one-sided since we only have Augustine's account. This is unfortunate since their debate was of considerable importance and produced reverberations which are still being felt today.

At root was the tension at the heart of the Christian faith between free will and determinism and specifically the question as to how far salvation is dependent on human decision and effort and how far on the grace of God. Pelagius has come to be stigmatised as a heretic because Augustine accused him of over-asserting the power of free will and diminishing the scope and power of divine grace. In fact, from what we are able to piece together from the few sources available, most of them filtered through Augustine's less than sympathetic eyes, it seems that the Celtic monk held to an orthodox view of the prevenience of God's grace and did not assert that individuals could achieve salvation purely by their own efforts. For him salvation was a matter of co-operation between nature and grace and not a matter of either one or the other. He argued that God's grace was freely available for all and that it was open to anyone to accept it. What he strongly and emphatically rejected was any notion of predestination or election and this was where he clashed with Augustine who held that to some extent God had already determined that some would achieve salvation and others would not. Pelagius found this idea wholly repellant and unacceptable. He believed strongly that God's offer of grace was universal and unconditional and that the choice lay entirely with individuals as to whether they accepted it or not.

He was equally unhappy with Augustine's stress on the doctrine of the fall and his notion of original sin as an inherited defect passed on from generation to generation like some universal hereditary disease. Augustine maintained that the smallest baby was inherently depraved and that if it died unbaptised it would go to Hell and suffer damnation. Pelagius found this idea of total depravity utterly repugnant and contrary to his whole understanding of God as a loving creator. Augustine quotes him as saying: 'Evil is not born with us and we are procreated without fault'. He felt that babies were born innocent and that baptism was a sign and seal of God's gracious love for them rather than an operation which had to be performed to avoid their dispatch to Hell.

Pelagius' position on both these issues almost certainly represented mainstream orthodoxy in both Eastern and Western Churches in the early Christian centuries. Rome, however, enthusiastically adopted Augustinianism with the result that the doctrines of predestination and original sin increasingly became the new orthodoxy in churches throughout Western Europe. Celtic Christians in the British Isles continued to cling to the more traditional and affirmative teachings about the human condition and as a result found themselves branded as Pelagian and the target of missionary sallies from Rome designed to purge them of their heretical beliefs. Palladius was probably sent to Ireland in 431 to counter Pelagian influences. He seems to have made little impact since the subsequent development of the Irish Church along monastic lines with a strong stress on asceticism, moral purity and seeking after perfection was very much in accordance with Pelagius' teaching. If anything, Christians on the British mainland were even more enthusiastically Pelagian. Germanus of Auxerre was sent over twice by the Pope in the mid-fifth century to disabuse them of their heretical views but once again he does not seem to have been very successful. Gildas reported that Pelagianism was still strong among the Welsh in the sixth century.

To some extent Pelagianism has remained the great British heresy – if, indeed, it really deserves that epithet. There has always been great concern in this country about good behaviour and individual morality. At times this can be taken to excessive lengths as Lord Macaulay observed in his famous statement that 'we know of no spectacle so ridiculous as the British public in one of its periodical fits of morality'. But there has also been a very positive side to this Pelagian stress on the way in which individuals live out their lives and respond to the unconditional offer of God's grace. The British have long taken the view that practical good works and charity are very important in the Christian life. The Epistle of James, which stresses good works and almost puts them on a par with faith as a prerequisite for salvation, has always been held in particular affection by Anglicans in marked contrast to its much more lukewarm reception by churches in other parts of Europe – Luther, it may be recalled, was so unhappy about its message that he wished it to be excluded from the New Testament canon. The doctrine of perfectionism, which suggests that in this world it is possible for individuals, dependent on and aided by grace, to attain ever higher levels of perfection has surfaced again and again in the British spiritual tradition – most notably in the hymns of the Wesley brothers where it is given perhaps its fullest expression in the line from Charles Wesley's 'Love divine, all loves excelling', 'Changed from glory into glory, till in heaven we take our place'.

There is another more fundamental aspect of the teaching of Pelagius and of the theology of Celtic Christianity as a whole which we would do well to re-examine today. It concerns the central Christian doctrine of the atonement. Christ's mission was seen not in terms of confronting an intrinsically corrupt world but rather of liberating an essentially good world from its bondage to evil forces. The Celts did not use the forbidding language of the courtroom which has so bedevilled both Roman Catholic and Protestant writing and preaching about the atonement. Words like ransom, advocate, justification and propitiation were alien to their thinking about Jesus Christ and his saving work. Rather they saw him primarily as the great liberator and emancipator, the one who draws us into the glorious liberty of the children of God. They saw him too very much as the *Christus Victor*, triumphant on the Cross having done battle with the Devil and won. This is an image which keeps recurring on their great high crosses. As we have seen, the Celts had a very real sense of the reality and power of sin and evil but these were regarded as external forces rather than as innate features of human nature. Along with the whole host of heaven, Christ had taken on these forces and defeated them and it was his victory and protection that was invoked in the breastplate prayers and the *caim*.

This is not to say that the idea of sacrifice was absent from the Celtic Christians' understanding of the atonement. On the contrary, it was central to their faith. But for them Christ's sacrifice was not viewed in pagan terms as the propitiation of an angry God nor in the forensic terms so popular in later Western theology as a ransom paid for sin. Rather they saw the Cross as a terrible but glorious mystery which pointed to the fact that life comes out of death and progress out of suffering. For them it was not just Jesus who suffered on the Cross but God himself. Indeed, their thinking strikingly anticipates the atonement theology developed in our own age by Jurgen Moltmann in his book *The Crucified God*. They saw God coming out of himself to humans and humans being carried out of themselves to God in response. In the words of Saunders Davies, 'This self-giving of God to mankind, evoking our self-giving to God is the essence of Celtic spirituality. It affirms that new life can only come out of sacrifice and suffering'.[9] It was this stress on self-sacrifice which underlay the three forms of martyrdom in Celtic monastic life and led so many to impose harsh physical disciplines on themselves, forsake their homes in favour of perpetual wandering and exile and follow the principles of the ascetic and moral life commended by Pelagius and others.

Pelagius may be the better known of the two great theologians of the Celtic Church but John Scotus Erigena was arguably the more influential. He has been described as the most powerful philosophical intellect in Western Europe between Augustine and Anselm.[10] Born in Ireland in the early years of the ninth century, he spent the latter part of his life in Laon, north east of Paris. Like Pelagius, his views landed him in serious trouble with the ecclesiastical authorities. The Synod of Valence in 855 accused him of pantheism and found him guilty of heresy. One of his main offences was his apparent denial of the objective existence of Hell. Like Pelagius he was extremely unhappy with the doctrine of predestination and in 851 he had written a treatise on the subject to counter the writings of a monk named Gottschalk who argued that God predestined some to damnation. Erigena found this idea logically as well as morally indefensible. God by his nature only willed what was good and it could not conceivably be any part of his plan that some should suffer eternal torment and misery. He went on to argue that the eternal fire of Hell was purely metaphorical; the punishment suffered by the wicked was not an objective physical reality but something that went on within their own minds. Like Milton in *Paradise Lost*, Erigena held that Heaven and Hell were not two separate places but rather reflected different perceptions of being in a state of extreme closeness to God. For some the divine light would shine with a life-enhancing warmth and colour, while for others it would have the quality of a blinding fire.

If Pelagius sought to establish the intrinsic goodness of human nature, Erigena was concerned with all nature and wanted to counter the damaging dualism which split God away from his creation and suggested that the material world was somehow profane and inferior to the spiritual. He expressed in philosophical form the Celts' sense of the immanence of God in creation. His two main works, which are still extant, were *Periphyseon*, or *De Divisione Naturae*, an extended meditation on the first chapter of Genesis, and a treatise on the Prologue to St John's Gospel. Both are strongly influenced by the theology of the Greek fathers. Indeed, Erigena is generally credited as the person who brought the whole Neo-Platonic philosophical tradition epitomised by Pseudo-Dionysius and Gregory of Nyssa to the West. In marked contrast to the Augustinian stress on original sin that now held sway in most of Europe, he held fast to the Greek idea that the material world was essentially good and that the natural destiny of all creation, including human beings, was to ascend to God through Christ.

Erigena adhered strongly to the Celtic view of the natural world as a theophany or showing of God's wonder and creativity. For him every object was a flash of the supernatural. God had not only made the world but to some extent he was the world, being not just the creator but also the essence of all things. Holding that 'making' was the same as 'being', he wrote, 'We ought not to understand God and the creatures as two things distinct from one another, but as one and the same. For both the creature, by subsisting, is in God; and God, by manifesting himself in a marvellous and ineffable manner, creates himself in creatures'.[11] It is not hard to see why he was accused of pantheism, although panentheism (seeing God as being in all creation but also as having an existence outside it) is a more accurate description of his position. He also came very close to espousing emanationism, the idea that all things proceed out of God, almost as a kind of extension of himself, and are destined to return into him. The principle of everything returning back to its source in God, which was a marked feature of Neo-Platonism, was particularly important to Erigena. He found it strongly confirmed in the opening verses of the Book of Ecclesiastes where there is a sense that for all the apparent vanity and futility of life there is a pattern with the sun and the wind returning to the place where they arose and rivers running into the sea which is yet never full. As he put it, 'Gyring in a gyre the Spirit goes forth and then comes back to its own place'. He was strongly attracted to the image of Christ as the Alpha and the Omega, the beginning and the end, the one who is both the pre-existent Logos that is the agent of creation and the one who will gather up all things and in whom all will be all. In a similar way he saw God as both the source and the fulfilment of all existence: 'He is the causal beginning of all those things, the essential middle which fulfils them and the end in which they are consummated and which brings all movement to rest'.[12]

In a fascinating way, the writings of this ninth century Celt anticipate one of the major theological movements of the late twentieth century. Process theologians share Erigena's sense of creation not as a once and for all event in the dim and distant past but as a continual ongoing process in which God is ever active, creating new life, perfecting what he has made and calling us back to him. They share too his emanationist leanings, holding that the very nature of God is to create and that the entire universe is in some senses an overflowing of his being and exists in an intimate and reciprocal relationship with him. These concepts are difficult to comprehend fully. Perhaps we can get nearest to understanding them by returning once again to the symbol of the Celtic knot with its constantly intertwining ribbons and spirals. There is the sense not only of continual movement and new creation but also of everything returning to the source from which it came. But the Celtic knot is not just a weary and futile round of constant repetition like the Buddhist *samsara*. It has a feeling of progress and direction, a linear thrust which transcends its circular pattern. It is full of suggestions of potentialities to be realised and possibilities to be encountered. Its progress is not easy or effortless – there are many detours and false trails to be pursued and superimposed on the pattern is the Cross of suffering and sacrifice. But there is a sense of everything fitting together, of the intimate intertwining of the material and the spiritual, humans and nature, God and the world, the Cross and creation.

Perhaps the most characteristically Celtic element in Erigena's thought was his abhorrence of division of any kind. He believed that if Christ stood for one thing above all it was the principle of reunion and that the purpose of his coming to earth was to heal the great divisions which had arisen within it. The tragedy of Western theology is that under the influence of Augustine and the Protestant Reformers it has sought to widen those divisions, seeking to separate the material from the spiritual, to distance humans from the rest of creation and to remove God from his creation. The effect of that dualism has been to produce an unhealthy over-concentration on sin and guilt and an attitude towards the natural world which has encouraged the reckless exploitation and pollution of our planet. We urgently need a return to those more holistic values of our Celtic ancestors which we so misguidedly abandoned. H. J. Massingham is surely justified in asserting in his book *The Tree of Life* that 'if the British Church had survived, it is possible that the fissure between Christianity and nature, widening through the centuries, would not have cracked the unity of western man's attitude to the universe'.[13] Noel O'Donoghue is equally not guilty of over-statement when he writes in his study *Patrick of Ireland*, 'The pessimism and anti-humanism of the later Augustine has cast a chilling gloom across Western Christendom. Only Celtic Christianity has entirely escaped this shadow. In this tradition men and women have opened to God and have trusted human nature in each other'.[14] As we begin to realise at last what we have lost in abandoning a faith that was firmly Christian yet holistic and affirmative of both human nature and the world around us, maybe we can still return to our own Celtic roots and rediscover the message of the intertwining ribbons of the Celtic knot.

4

Monks and Pilgrims

Mention the word church nowadays and most people will probably think of solid stone buildings with spires and stained glass windows. Depending on their denominational background, they may well think too of a highly organised structure of presbyteries, dioceses, circuits or synods. The Celtic Church had none of these features. Indeed, as I suggested in Chapter 1, it is perhaps a mistake to refer to it as a church at all. The Celts had no great taste for ecclesiology or organisation and expressed their faith through communities which were essentially temporary and provisional. Their places of worship were rarely if ever constructed of stone, sometimes of wood but much more often simply of wattle and daub. Although there were settled parish ministers serving a distinct geographical area they were eclipsed in number and importance by the monks and pilgrims who wandered from place to place. The dominant institution of Celtic Christianity was neither the parish church nor the cathedral but the monastery, which sometimes began as a solitary hermit's cell and often grew to become a combination of commune, retreat house, mission station, hotel, hospital, school, university, arts centre and powerhouse for the local community – a source not just of spiritual energy but also of hospitality, learning and cultural enlightenment.

Celtic monasteries varied enormously in size and composition. Some consisted of a few simple huts or cells and were essentially places of retreat and solitude. Others grew to resemble small townships with well over a thousand monks. Within their walls, which were designed to keep domestic animals in rather than strangers out, the sexes mixed freely.

There were married and celibate monks, and women as well as men took the monastic vow. It was not unusual for women to preside over mixed monasteries as St Hilda did at Whitby and St Ita at Killeedy in Limerick. Monastic life centred around prayer, study and manual labour although it was not governed by a strict rule of the kind imposed by St Benedict. The community gathered together several times a day for services and to chant psalms. In between monks pursued private prayer and study, worked in the gardens and fields, taught pupils or copied manuscripts. The variety of their life is well brought out in a poem attributed to St Columba:

> That I might bless the Lord
> Who orders all;
> Heaven with its countless bright orders,
> Land, strand and flood,
> That I might search in all the books
> That would help my soul;
> At times kneeling to the Heaven of my heart,
> At times singing psalms;
> At times contemplating the King of Heaven,
> Chief of the Holy Ones;
> At times at work without compulsion,
> This would be delightful.
> At times plucking duilisc from the rocks
> At other times fishing
> At times distributing food to the poor
> At times in a hermitage.[1]

As this poem indicates, it was quite usual for Celtic monks to alternate between periods of administrative or manual work in the monastery and times of solitary contemplation in a hermit's cell. Many also spent several years as missionaries or pilgrims wandering from place to place. But although both solitude and pilgrimage were important features of Celtic spirituality, so too was community. One of the reasons why monasteries became the dominant institution of Celtic Christianity was because their espousal of communal values struck a deep chord in a tribal society where ties of family and kinship were strong. They reinforced that strong sense of the importance of community which is conveyed by the Welsh word *llan* and which has made the concept of personal possession or individual ownership quite alien to the Irish language. The phrase used is rather *mo cuid*, meaning 'my portion' and indicating that the world's goods exist for the benefit of all and that each person takes his or her share on the basis of need and without any thought of acquiring material things for their own sake. The same sentiment is, of course, strongly conveyed in the line from 'Be thou my vision': 'Riches I heed not, nor man's empty praise'.

As well as sharing and leading a communal lifestyle, Celtic monks also pursued self-denial and submitted themselves to severe physical deprivations and punishments. An ascetic discipline prevailed and three forms of martyrdom were commended. Red martyrdom involved enduring persecution for Christ's sake, white martyrdom meant abandoning everything one loved for God and green martyrdom consisted of freeing oneself from evil desires by fasting, hard labour or physically demanding forms of prayer. Monks often spent many hours practising the cross vigil, with their arms fully extended and hands raised up to heaven. Genuflections were common, the daily average being about 200 although one anchorite at Clonard was said to have got down on his knees 700 times a day. One of the most distinctive literary products of Irish monasticism is the penitential, a detailed list of severe punishments for every conceivable misdemeanour. Penance was looked on as a sign of sincerity and was strictly enforced. Corporal punishment was common and so too were long periods of fasting. In addition to the ordinary season of Lent, which they called the Lent of Jesus, Irish monks also observed the Lent of Elias in winter and the Lent of Moses after Pentecost. Even at the best of times meals were generally sparse and meat was seldom if ever served. Some abbots permitted beer to be taken with meals but this was by no means universal. Maelruin did not allow any drink at Tallaght on the grounds that he would 'never let anything that makes the brothers forget God pass their lips'. Dugla, abbot of the sister monastery at Finglas where it was permitted, once ventured to suggest that his monks would get to heaven just the same. 'They may not get there quite as quickly as mine' was Maelruin's reply.[2]

Those practising such a demanding lifestyle needed support. Even hermits pursuing the solitary life in remote cells and caves had spiritual directors or soul friends with whom they regularly met to unburden themselves and seek direction. These soul friends, or *anamchairde* as they were called in Irish, were among the most important and distinctive figures in the Celtic Church. They combined the roles of spiritual director, guru, confessor and confidential counsellor. For the monks they were of particular importance – many abbots acknowledged that it was more important to follow one's soul friend than obey the monastic rules – but they were also much used by the laity. One of the most famous sayings from the Celtic Christian world, attributed variously to St Comgall, St Brigid and others, is that a person without a soul friend is like a body without a head. To some extent this was another example of the baptising by Christians of a practice that had been common among pagan Celts whereby every chief had his own Druid counsellor. St Patrick is said to have replaced Dubthach, a Druid, as the adviser to Laogaire, the high king of the Irish. But in their Christian incarnation soul friends were not just a feature of high society, nor were they drawn from the priestly caste. Indeed, it seems to have been more common for lay men and women to perform the role. Modern experts in the field of spiritual counselling and clinical psychology are coming to see the advantages of this Celtic model of pastoral care which faced up to the need we all have for regularly unburdening our souls without having to resort to the formal ritual or the guilt-inducing aspects of the confessional. Interestingly, a recent book on spirituality and pastoral care by Kenneth Leech has the title *Soul Friend*.

The Celtic monasteries were not just religious institutions in the narrow sense. They opened their doors to seekers and scholars of all kinds and became important centres of learning and culture. In this respect they took over the role which had been fulfilled by communities of bards and *filid* in pre-Christian times. Several monasteries seem to have been founded on the sites of such pagan centres of learning and it has been suggested that in some cases fraternities of Druid scholars were converted *en masse* and their colleges turned into monasteries with virtually no upheaval or dislocation. Certainly the culture and learning fostered in the Celtic monasteries during the so-called Dark Ages was broad and had a secular as well as a religious context. If the monks had a scriptural inspiration for their work, it was surely St Paul's injunction to the Philippians to hold on to whatsoever things are pure and lovely and good. This meant keeping alive native traditions of poetry and folksong as well as copying the Scriptures, practising the art of manuscript illumination, studying classical authors both for their philosophy and their theology and fashioning exquisite brooches and rings. Irish monasteries, less troubled by Anglo-Saxon and Viking interference than those on mainland Britain, were particularly renowned both for their scholarship and their discipline. Bede recounts that many Englishmen

> left their own country and retired to Ireland either for the sake of religious studies or to live a more ascetic life. In course of time some of these devoted themselves faithfully to the monastic life, while others preferred to travel round to the cells of various teachers and apply themselves to study. The Irish welcomed them all gladly, gave them their daily food, and also provided them with books to read and with instruction, without asking for any payment.[3]

The monasteries also had an important role as centres for mission. It was from Iona and Lindisfarne that most of Scotland and the North of England were effectively evangelised. Monks were sent out in twos and threes to establish what Columba called 'colonies of heaven' within a land that was largely pagan. The way that they worked was very different from the approach of later Christian missionaries who joined forces with traders and imperial adventurers and sought to impose their own Western values and secure a cultural as well as a religious conversion of the natives. There is a danger of over-romanticising this aspect of Celtic Christianity, as of so many others. As I pointed out in Chapter 1, there may well have been an element of calculation and even sometimes of political intrigue in the evangelistic activities of men like

Columba. That said, however, the approach of the Celtic missionaries was essentially gentle and sensitive. They sought to live alongside the people with whom they wanted to share the good news of Christ, to understand and to respect their beliefs and not to dominate or culturally condition them.

Celtic missionaries were not so much engaged in 'converting' heathens as in incorporating them into the Christian fold. As we have seen, they found much within the existing pagan religion to admire and to baptise: the sense of the divine presence in nature and respect for the physical environment, the strong understanding of community and attachment to culture and learning, the stress on morality and active charity. Here, indeed, Christ already dwelt even if he was not recognised as such. David Adam puts it very well: 'The Celtic church did not so much seek to bring Christ as to discover Him: not to possess Him, but to see Him in "friend and stranger"; to liberate the Christ who is already there in all his riches'.[4]

There is surely something for us to learn from here at a time when once again the Church in Britain, as across the whole Western world, is operating in a society which is largely pagan and where there are many different faiths. John Harvey, a Church of Scotland minister who has spent most of his time working in deprived inner city areas and is now leader of the Iona Community, believes that the Celts' approach to mission has much to offer to us today. He sees their monasteries as being similar to the base Christian communities of contemporary Latin America – small, flexible, rooted in particular communities and situations, with a strong sense of corporate discipline, centering on a ministry of Word and sacrament which are not the preserve of a priestly caste but are available to the whole people. He feels that it is these kinds of small cells and communities, increasingly springing up in many parts of the world, that will be a better tool for Christian mission in the future than the older and more institutional churches:

When I think of the missionary outreach of the Celtic Church in the sixth and seventh centuries, I think of monks going out from Iona in their twos and threes in their wee coracles and travelling across the sea into darkest Germany and living there in amongst the Germanic tribes, taking over the sacred groves of these tribes and trying to help them see that the gods of wood and stone that they were worshipping pointed beyond themselves to the one God who was the living God. Now they didn't go in there and simply ignore the culture of their time, nor did they go in there and collude with it. There was a balance – a critical involvement. Now it seems to me that's a very good model for missionary activity today where you have little groups of people witnessing to the Gospel by their way of life, living together whether it be in a high rise flat in the inner-city, on a housing estate or in a house in the suburbs.

Isn't this a good way of gossiping the gospel around the streets among folk who are three or four generations away from any connection with the Christian church, secular materialists? How are we going to reach these people with the good news of the Gospel and enable them to respond in their own terms if we don't both share in the culture of their times and of their street and at the same time have a critical involvement with it? I think that is what the Celtic missionary monks did and I think that's what we have to do today.[5]

Missionary zeal was one of the reasons why Celtic monks travelled so much throughout the British Isles and the Continent. Their urge to follow the pilgrims' way also had other more complex spiritual roots. Nowadays the word pilgrimage conjures up images of people visiting holy places and shrines, often in the hope of gaining a miraculous cure or experiencing some special spiritual benefit. This kind of travel was not unknown among Celtic Christians. There was a regular traffic of monks and others to Jerusalem and Rome, though a verse said to have been penned by an Irish monk testifies to the high degree of scepticism that prevailed about the spiritual benefits to be obtained from such trips.

Who to Rome goes
Much labour, little profit knows;

For God, on earth though long you've sought him,
You'll miss at Rome unless you've brought him.[6]

The almost perpetual state of wandering which characterised the lives of many Celtic monks and saints was in part
an aspect of their asceticism and desire to follow the path of
renunciation and self-denial. Pilgrimage was conceived of as
a kind of perpetual exile from the comforts and distractions
of home. It often seems to have been undertaken as a penance,
sometimes on the suggestion of a soul friend or confessor.
Peregrinatio was described as 'seeking the place of one's resurrection'. So it undoubtedly was for St Columba. There are
various stories about why he left his beloved Donegal and set
out across the Irish Sea with twelve companions. Some suggest that he was doing penance for his involvement in a
bloody battle, others that he had offended another monk by
copying a book. Adamnan, the Saint's biographer, simply
tells us that he quit his native shores '*pro Christo peregrinari
volens*', desiring to be a pilgrim for Christ. Whatever the reason
for his voyage he seems to have seen it as a kind of exile.
Some stories suggest the party first landed on the island of
Oronsay but Columba insisted that they could not stay there
because Ireland was still visible. The first thing that he did
when they got to Iona was to climb its highest hill and assure
himself that he could not see his beloved homeland from it.
To this day the hill is known in Gaelic as *Carn Cul Ri Eirinn*
(Hill of the Turning Back to Ireland). A deep sense of longing
for his native land and its people pervades many of the poems
and prayers that he composed on Iona. St Patrick also chose
a life of exile, forsaking his home on the British mainland to
spend his adult life in the country which he had known only
as a slave.

There was, of course, a clear scriptural impulse behind this
desire for exile and pilgrimage. The Celts were consciously
responding to Our Lord's oft-repeated call to his disciples to
leave home and family and follow him. They were also mind-
ful of the fact that Jesus himself had led a wandering and
unsettled existence and of his remark that 'the foxes have
holes, and the birds of the air have nests; but the Son of man
hath nowhere to lay his head' (Matt. 8:20). Perhaps an even

more direct influence was the Old Testament narrative of the journey of an exiled people through the wilderness and the desert. Many Celtic saints had God's words to Abraham ringing in their ears as they took up their staffs and set out on their own pilgrimages: 'Get thee out of thy country, and from thy kindred, and from thy father's house, unto a land that I will shew thee' (Gen. 12:1).

Not that it was to lands flowing with milk and honey that the Celtic pilgrims took themselves. They often sought out the most desolate, isolated, barren places, staying there a while in their simple beehive cells before moving on again. Here another influence was clearly at work: the example of the desert fathers like St Antony who had established a pattern of discipleship based on withdrawal from the world and solitary contemplation. The idea of the desert was very important in Celtic Christianity as can be seen from the number of places which bear the name Dysart in Scotland, Dysserth or Dyserth in Wales and Diseart in Ireland. Lacking the barren sandy wildernesses of Egypt and Syria, Celtic monks made for the most barren and remote spots in the British Isles. They found their own deserts on islands like Skellig Michael, the rocky promontory twelve miles off the south west tip of the Kerry coast which is still honeycombed with beehive cells, and Bardsey, off the Lleyn Peninsula in North Wales, inaccessible for much of the winter yet known as the burial place of 20,000 saints.

Retreat to these desert places often followed a period of intense missionary activity or involvement in the administrative affairs of a busy monastery. Celtic religious life balanced periods of activity with times of complete withdrawal. Columbanus, who spent most of his life wandering across Europe establishing monasteries, regularly withdrew into a cave for periods of fifty days or more. Fursey, after preaching for ten years in Ireland, retreated to a tiny island where he lived alone for a while before embarking on a hectic missionary tour of East Anglia. Then he retreated again to Gaul and spent a further period as a solitary. St Paulin started his monastic life in Wales as a hermit, influenced by St Antony and the desert tradition, and then had a busy period evangelising Cornwall before, in his biographer's words, 'being on fire with longing for perfection, the idea occurred to him of leaving the land of his fathers and crossing the sea to foreign lands where he might live unknown to all save God alone'. He spent his last years on earth as a hermit in Brittany, fasting and leading a life of considerable austerity. Many monks shared the craving for retreat and solitude in the face of approaching death described in this ninth century Irish poem:

> All solitary in my little cell,
> With not a single soul as company;
> That would be a pilgrimage dear to me
> Before going to the meeting with death.[7]

As well as these specifically spiritual motives, a more general *wanderlust* almost certainly underlay the constant travels and wanderings of so many Celtic Christians. The Celts as a race had always been on the move, spreading gradually westwards across Europe from their central European heartland. Although they were not nomadic, they were certainly restless and inveterate travellers. Their instincts when they got somewhere were not, like the Romans or the Normans, to colonise and rule it, nor like the Vikings to pillage and raid it. Rather they lived lightly on the land, adapting themselves to the local culture and establishing structures that were provisional and temporary. Voyaging was in their blood. The great epic sagas of Celtic literature tell of journeys to fabulous lands. One of the best known, the Voyage of Bran which dates from the seventh or eighth century, describes a long sea voyage inspired by a call which the hero hears in magical music. Bran visits many islands, including the Island of Birds and the Island of Women until he finally reaches the Island of Joy. As with so much else in pagan Celtic culture, this story was Christianised in the ninth century to become the Voyage of St Brendan which describes a seven-year search for the Island of the Saints, the land of promise which the hero has been told about by an aged monk. On the way Brendan encounters many other islands, including, like Bran, an island of birds. Eventually he comes to his destination, only to find that in reality the end of the voyage is death and to be told that 'the Lord Jesus Christ did not allow you to find it immediately because first he wished to show you the richness of his wonders in the deep'.[8]

Embedded deep in the Celtic psyche was the sense that it is better to travel hopefully than to arrive. There was a feeling too that the grass was always greener, and maybe God was also nearer, across the waters or on the other side of the hill. This kind of restlessness sometimes provoked a sharp rebuke. The Abbess of Clonbroney once told a would-be pilgrim, 'Were God to be found overseas, I too would take ship and go. But since God is near to all that call upon him, there is no constraint upon us to seek him overseas. For from every land there is a way to the kingdom of Heaven'.[9] Such admonitions, however, did little to quell the Celts' *wanderlust*. Much more typical is the oft-quoted story of the three monks who set off from the south of Ireland in a coracle without oars or proper provisions and drifted across the sea for seven days before being beached on the north coast of Cornwall. Brought before King Alfred who questioned them as to why they had come, they replied disarmingly, 'We stole away because we wanted for the love of God to be on pilgrimage, we cared not where'.

The Celts themselves were well aware of the difference between genuine *peregrinatio* and the restlessness and escapism to which they were prone as a race. The Book of Lismore, a medieval Irish compilation of the lives of the saints, distinguishes three kinds of pilgrimage. The first, leaving one's country in a physical sense but with no inner change of heart, is dismissed as a waste of time and energy. The second, earnestly desiring to leave everything familiar and comfortable behind and embark on a life of pilgrimage but being forced by pressing duties to remain at home, is recognised as a worthy calling. The third, leaving one's country for God and forsaking a life of comfort and ease for one of austerity and virtue, is regarded as the highest calling of all.

This stress on the importance of the inner journey of repentance, resurrection and rebirth brings us to the heart of the Celtic idea of pilgrimage. *Peregrinatio* was the outward expression of an inner change, a metaphor and symbol for that journey towards deeper faith and greater holiness and towards God which is the Christian life. To be a pilgrim was to live in imitation of Jesus, to take up his cross and to recognise that in this transitory world we have no abiding city. Perhaps no one articulated this view better than Columbanus, whose own wanderings across Europe were accompanied by frequent meditations on the theme of pilgrimage in the Christian life. Again and again in his sermons he likens life to a road or a journey and points to the dangers of being distracted by the way and mistaking it for the ultimate destination.

A road to life art thou, not Life . . . And there is no man makes his dwelling on the road, but walks there: and those who fare along the road have their dwelling in the fatherland. So thou art naught, O mortal life, naught but a road, a fleeting ghost, an emptiness, a cloud uncertain and frail, a shadow and a dream . . .

Therefore let us concern ourselves with heavenly things and not human ones, and like pilgrims always sigh for our homeland, long for our homeland. It is the end of the road that travellers look for and desire, and because we are travellers and pilgrims through this world, it is the road's end, that is of our lives, that we should always be thinking about. For that road's end is our true homeland. Don't let us love the road more than the land to which it leads, lest we lose our homeland altogether. For we have such a homeland that we ought to love it.

So then, while we are on the road, as travellers, as pilgrims, as guests of the world, let us not get entangled with any earthly desires and lusts but fill our minds with heavenly and spiritual things; our theme song 'When shall I come and appear before the face of my God?'[10]

This could seem a rather morbid and gloomy creed which sees little good in this life and looks to death as the only thing worth prizing. Columbanus does come close to expressing this view in his writings. 'I shall hasten towards death', he says in one sermon, 'that there I may see sure things and true, and all things together in one, which is impossible for me here'.[11] Celtic Christians took seriously Christ's strictures about laying up treasures on earth where moth and rust will corrupt them. They had a very clear sense of the transience and impermanence of this life and of our status in this world being that of pilgrims and strangers. But we should not forget too their clear feel for the essential goodness of the world, their enjoyment of the beauties of creation and their positive and affirmative view of nature, including human nature. They were not people who hated the world and denied its power to lift the human spirit and raise it to God.

The idea of pilgrimage is one that we badly need to recover today. Contemporary Christianity can be dangerously static. Too often we make the mistake of thinking that life and faith work on the same principle as the pantomime with a sudden transformation scene changing everything miraculously and effortlessly. The story of Cinderella should remind us that even in pantomimes the transition from rags to ball gown is only temporary and the golden coach turns back into a pumpkin at the stroke of midnight. Most of us are not the recipients of sudden blinding flashes of spiritual light which change our lives for ever and signal that no further effort is required on our part. We are often very reluctant to accept that faith is something that develops and grows gradually and which involves taking risks and being prepared to follow detours and false trails as we seek out the right way. The example of our Celtic Christian forebears can surely help us to keep on going and not to stop because we feel that we have made it to the end of our journey. They remind us that in this life at least the journey is never quite over. Theirs is the message that Sydney Carter has so brilliantly taken up in his song 'One more step along the world I go' with its portrayal of our lives and our faith as a journey from the old world to the new in which Jesus travels along with us. It is also the theme of that familiar passage which opens the twelfth chapter of the Epistle to the Hebrews: 'Wherefore seeing we also are encompassed about with so great a cloud of witnesses, let us lay aside every weight, and the sin which doth so easily beset us, and let us run with patience the race that is set before us, looking unto Jesus the author and finisher of our faith'.

Like the author of those words, the Celtic Christians believed Jesus to be the Alpha and the Omega, the beginning and the end of the journey. Like him too they felt that all who were genuine travellers and seekers on the way of faith were encompassed and protected by a great heavenly host. Their idea of pilgrimage can perhaps be best understood by going back yet again to the intertwining ribbons and ever curving spirals of the Celtic knot. What is particularly striking about them is their sense of constant movement. The lines may constantly double back on each other and return where they started but the overall impression is of a purposeful progress rather than a random meandering or a vain and frustrating repetition. There are many detours and diversions but ultimately there is a sense of surely and securely reaching a destination. If that destination is in fact to arrive back at the same place where we started then that is to recognise with T. S. Eliot that 'What we call the beginning is often the end and to make an end is to make a beginning. The end is where we start from.' The Celtic knot, like Celtic Christianity as a whole, urges us to travel hopefully on our way as pilgrims together.

> We shall not cease from exploration
> And the end of all our exploring
> Will be to arrive where we started
> And know the place for the first time.[12]

5
The Power of Imagination

Two powerful if contradictory trends threaten the integrity and perhaps even the survival of contemporary Western Christianity. One would turn it into a highly abstract and conceptualised academic discipline appealing only to intellectuals while the other would reduce it to a series of shallow emotional slogans. In both cases what is at risk is an understanding of the element of mystery which is at the heart of the Christian faith.

As we face this dual threat from overdeveloped intellectualism and overdeveloped emotionalism, Celtic Christianity may offer us a lifeline in the form of an approach to faith which is rooted in the imagination. Celtic Christians were not anti-intellectual. They produced at least two leading theologians and had a passion for learning and culture. Nor did they disdain the emotional side of Christianity – there is a clear appeal to the heart in their prayers and poems. But perhaps their most marked characteristic was their power of imagination. They excelled at expressing their faith in symbols, metaphors and images, both visual and poetic. They had the ability to invest the ordinary and the commonplace with sacramental significance, to find glimpses of God's glory throughout creation and to paint pictures in words, signs and music that acted as icons opening windows on heaven and pathways to eternity. As such, they have much to teach Christians today seeking to rekindle their imaginative faculties and recover what has perhaps been the most neglected aspect of growth and development in the faith.

A good example of the application of this Celtic power of imagination is the story of St Patrick's encounter with the

Irish princesses recounted in Chapter 2. His use of a shamrock to explain the doctrine of the Trinity is paralleled by an early Irish verse which uses similar everyday imagery to approach this central Christian mystery.

Three folds of the cloth, yet only one napkin is there,
Three joints in the finger, but still only one finger fair;
Three leaves of the shamrock, yet no more than one
    shamrock to wear,
Frost, snow-flakes and ice, all in water their origin share,
Three Persons in God; to one God alone we make prayer.[1]

This is the spirituality of a people who perceive with their senses rather than their intellect or emotions. The Celts, of course, inhabited a misty world of dreams, visions and pre-monitions. But it was also a world where people opened their eyes to see and their ears to hear what was around them. Donald Allchin, an English clergyman, has written much about this aspect of Celtic spirituality and feels that it has an important message for us today. His book on the Welsh spiritual tradition, *Praise Above All*, commends the Welsh word *synhwyrus* which means 'perceived by the senses'. In conversation with me he elaborated on what he finds both distinctive and relevant today about this particular dimension of the Celtic imagination: 'It's something to do with a statement of the faith which is in images and not in concepts. We've had over-conceptual forms of Christianity in the West over the last 400 years, fighting one another and getting more and more abstract as they did so. Here is a way of stating the Christian faith which is almost entirely in terms of images – poetic images and visual images. In this sense, of course, it is also very close to Coptic and Syriac Christianity which also deal primarily in images'.[2]

We can never, of course, enter fully into the Celtic imagination. Our senses have been too blunted by the mass media and the crude commercial pressures of modern consumer society. But if we cannot hope to recapture its fresh innocence and sense of open wonder, we can at least appreciate and learn from the products of that imagination that have been passed down to us – the prayers and poems, the songs and works of art. Perhaps the most striking of these surviving Celtic icons are the great high standing crosses scattered throughout Ireland and across West Wales and the Western Isles of Scotland. Standing up to fifteen feet high, their faces decorated with biblical scenes, carvings of birds and animals and the interweaving pattern of the Celtic knot, they powerfully express some of the dominant themes of Celtic Christianity – incorporation of pagan ideas and images, love of nature, integration of creation and redemption and the centrality of the Cross.

Archaeologists are now generally agreed that Celtic crosses were a development from the standing stones of pre-Christian cults which are so marked a feature of the British landscape from Stonehenge in the south to Callanish on the island of Lewis in the north. Some of these pagan stones, which had possibly been erected to symbolise the link between earth and heaven, were baptised by Christian Celts by the act of drawing the symbol of a fish on their surface. There are examples of such carved stones at Edderton, near Tain in Rosshire in the north of Scotland, and at Fuerty in Roscommon, Ireland. The distinctive shape of the Celtic Cross, ringed with a circle around its arms, seems to have developed from a design which incorporated the first two letters of Christ's name in Greek – *Chi* (X) and *Rho* (P). It was by combining these two letters that the symbol of the ringed cross seems to have emerged. This development can be traced on the so-called 'cross slabs' or recumbent stones found in the north east of Scotland, notably at Monymusk in Aberdeenshire and Skinnet and Ulbster in Caithness. The designs on them have a close affinity to symbols found on stones at Whithorn and provide strong evidence to support the theory that either St Ninian himself or later monks from *Candida Casa* were active among the Picts in North East Scotland.

The process of development and refinement which transformed these rough slabs with their crudely drawn *Chi Rho* symbols into ornately carved high standing crosses took many centuries. At some point, probably in Ireland in the second half of the seventh century, the standing stones 'sprouted wings' and were given cross arms encircled by a ring. It is this kind of cross that reached the islands off the west coast of Scotland – notably Iona, where three fine examples can be seen in front of the restored abbey and Islay where the Kildalton Cross remains in a remarkable state of preservation. Several of the Welsh crosses reveal a different process of development with a solid wheel-head cross being fixed on top of a long shaft covered in carvings of interlacing and key patterns.

It was in Ireland that this branch of Celtic Christian art reached its highest level of development. More than 200 high standing crosses can still be seen there, the great majority constructed between the seventh and twelfth centuries and revealing a wealth of decorative detail and spiritual imagination. The most striking examples are at Monasterboice near Drogheda and at Moone to the south west of Dublin. Their exquisitely carved panels illustrate familiar biblical stories and also portray images from the world of nature. At their focal points are scenes representing the Last Judgement or Christ in glory on the Cross. The meaning of some of the more abstract designs is much less clear, as in the case of the oft-repeated swastika-like pattern made up of the intertwining bodies of four elongated human figures or serpents. As I have already mentioned, there have been a number of different scholarly interpretations of the symbolism of the circle which surrounds the cross arms and gives the Celtic cross its characteristic shape. Some see it as representing the sun and so incorporating both Druid and Christian objects of worship in a single syncretistic symbol. Others take it to stand for the globe of the earth and to suggest the interrelationship of creation and redemption. It has also been interpreted as symbolising the circle of eternity, the position of Jesus as the Alpha and Omega, and as the wreath and the crown of the *Christus Victor*.

It is a tribute to the power and depth of this imagery that it lends itself to so many different interpretations. But we need to beware of over-analysing the symbolism of the Celtic crosses. Their purpose may have been very simple – to act as a focal point for people to gather for outdoor worship, to illustrate and point up particular stories and themes in the Bible and Christian teaching, rather in the manner of picture books, posters and videos today, and perhaps also to stand as stone versions of the *lorica* or breastplate prayers invoking God's protection on the local community. John Sharkey, an Irish writer now living in Wales who has made a special study of Celtic crosses, put to me the dangers of over-interpreting their meaning as we stood looking at the particularly fine example which stands in the churchyard at Nevern in Pembrokeshire: 'When we approach these crosses nowadays and look closely and try and work out what all the patterns mean and how they interrelate with each other, we lose an overall sense of what they were put up for. They weren't meant to be talked about in terms of aesthetics but to symbolise Christ and the Crucifixion. They were put up literally to stop people in their tracks'.[3]

There is a lot to be said for subjugating our desire to be amateur archaeologists and art critics, forever tracing influences and finding meanings, and allowing these surviving icons from deep in our collective past to stop us in our tracks. Pierced by the sun's rays or silhouetted against the evening sky the high crosses still have an enormous power and presence, standing as silent witnesses to the eternal that is in our midst and pointing from earth to heaven. The illuminated manuscripts that are the other great artistic legacy of the Celtic Church can exert a similar spiritual power. Too often we treat them primarily as tourist attractions on a par with secular works of art, queuing up to enter the room in Trinity College, Dublin, where the best of them are preserved, marvelling at their glowing colours and intricate detail and then visiting the adjoining shop to buy headscarfs, sweatshirts, children's colouring-in books and posters adorned with their patterns and motifs. What we are in danger of forgetting is that they were created for spiritual rather than aesthetic purposes, not as paintings to be gazed on in galleries but as objects of meditation and windows into the mystery and glory of God.

The oldest extant illuminated manuscript gives us a direct link with the very early days of the Celtic Church in Britain. It is the so-called Cathach of St Columba, a psalter dating from the mid sixth century which is said to have been a copy made by Columba of a book which he borrowed without permission from another monk. It has even been suggested that it was the subsequent row over this incident that led to him quitting Ireland for Iona. The names given to manuscripts are often confusing and reflect their ultimate home rather than their place of origin. The Lichfield Gospels were actually compiled in Llandeilo in Wales, the Book of Durrow was probably produced in Northumberland and taken to the Irish monastery which now bears its name for safe keeping during a period of Viking raids, while the Stowe Missal was produced in Tallaght in the early ninth century and found its way to England many centuries later when it was bought by the Duke of Buckingham.

The Book of Kells, rightly regarded as the supreme example of the art of Celtic manuscript illumination, also has a deceptive name. Almost certainly produced on Iona in the late eighth or early ninth century, it was taken to the Irish monastry of Kells to escape being pillaged by Vikings. Thought to be the work of many hands, it has been estimated that the skins of around 150 calves must have been needed for its vellum pages. Virtually every one of the 340 pages which survive is illustrated in vivid colours. The influence of Egyptian and Coptic Christian art can be seen in the icon-like portraits of the Virgin and Child and of Christ with their exaggeratedly large heads and unnatural bodies. The distinctive motif of the Celtic knot recurs again and again, made up not just of intertwining ribbons but also snakes, elongated animals and human bodies. The illustrations are full of spiritual symbols like the image of a butterfly escaping from a chrysalis used to signify the soul's escape from the body. Of particular significance is the lozenge shape which occupies the focal point of both the *Chi Rho* page illustrating St Matthew's description of the birth of Christ and the page of symbols which opens St John's Gospel. It has been widely interpreted as representing the *Logos* or Incarnation. In the portrait of St John a lozenge decorates the Gospel book held by the evangelist while on the page illustrating the Virgin and Child the same shape is found on a brooch worn by the Virgin.

Religious symbolism also characterises the intricate metalwork produced by the Christian Celts. The Ardagh Chalice, an exquisitely delicate piece of filigree work dating from the early eighth century and found by a boy digging in a field in the 1860s, is now displayed in the National Museum of Antiquities in Dublin. Scholars have pointed to the significance of numbers which are found represented on it. The girdle running between its two handles has twelve gold filigree patterns, punctuated by twelve blue and red studs – a reference to the apostles. The number eight also figures prominently in the decoration on the underside of the chalice. This is taken to refer to the day of the resurrection since Christ rose on the eighth day. Deeper and more complex symbolism has also been detected in the decoration of the chalice and of other surviving pieces of Celtic metalwork.

As with the crosses, there is a danger that we can overanalyse and interpret Celtic manuscript illumination and decorative metalwork. Subtle and profound though the imagery often is, there is also a quality of directness and naivety which it is all too easy to dismiss as primitive and immature. The Celts' apparent inability to draw in perspective and their strangely distorted representations of humans and animals have tended to offend cultured Western sensibilities schooled in classical and Renaissance principles. In the late twentieth century, however, we are much more attuned to primitive and non-representational art and as a result we are in a much better position to appreciate the abstract imagery of Celtic design than previous generations. Our so-called post modern culture may also find it easier to tune into those deeper rhythms and cadences of Celtic spirituality which were expressed in a distinctive style of music.

As Noel O'Donoghue has eloquently observed, the Celts were deeply conscious of rhythm:

> the rhythms of human life and the body's ages and changes, the rhythms of the seasons, of work such as weaving and milking, of reaping with hook or scythe, of threshing the corn, of men rowing together, of women walking together. All these rhythms, and many others, were vocalised in song and what was called *port beul* or voice music.[4]

The Celts sang as they worked, as they played and as they prayed. In Gaelic there is no word for music that is not sung while in Welsh the word for poetry and music is the same.

As in so many other areas, there was a clear continuity between pagan and Christian song. Fairy lullabies were adapted to become lullabies to the Christ child and the distinctive *caoines*, deep murmuring laments based on the mournful call of the redshank and involving constant repetition of the name of the deceased, became mourning hymns.

The music that survives from the early Celtic Church has a deeply rhythmic and repetitive quality that is almost hypnotic. Bells seem to have played an important role in the lives of monks and pilgrims. One of the earliest still extant bears St Adamnan's name and was quite possibly rung by him as he travelled from Iona across mainland Scotland spreading the Gospel. It was recently heard on the excellent BBC Radio Scotland series *Scotland's Music*, as was the bell-like sound produced by striking the remarkably resonant rock in Brittany associated with St Gildas. The same series, compiled by John Purser, also featured items from the only surviving collection of Celtic Church music, the Inchcolm Antiphoner, a twelfth century manuscript from the abbey of Inchcolm which stood on an island in the Firth of Forth. Its plainsong chants celebrating the life of St Columba, to whom the abbey was dedicated, may well go back to the seventh century. Although recognisably in the tradition of monastic plainchant they have a more lyrical, mystical, sinuous quality than the cooler and more controlled Gregorian chant favoured by Rome. Listening to them in the commercial recording that has now been made by the Scottish choral group Capella Nova it is not difficult to appreciate why several musicologists believe that it was in the Celtic world, and possibly in Ireland, that polyphony originated.

While the choirs of Inchcolm and other monasteries were producing plainsong of a greater complexity and delicacy than that found in the great Benedictine foundations of the Middle Ages, ordinary Celtic Christians were singing their faith in a simpler and more elemental way. In the introduction to *Carmina Gadelica* Alexander Carmichael gives a fascinating description of the way in which the people of the Outer Hebrides recited their prayers in the late nineteenth century. The practice that he writes about almost certainly went back to the sixth century and reflects a tradition that takes in St

91

David, the waterman, wading out into the sea off Pembroke-shire to chant his psalms and St Cuthbert standing in the North Sea with his otters. Prayers and runes were chanted, Carmichael noted,

> in low tremulous unmeasured cadences like the moving and moaning, the soughing and sighing of the ever-murmuring sea on their old wild shores . . . I have known men and women of eighty, ninety and a hundred years of age con-tinue the practice of their lives in going from one to two miles to the seashore to join their voices with the voicing of the waves and their praises with the praises of the cease-less sea.[5]

This kind of mouth music, so deeply in tune with the rhythms of nature, is very different from the four-square hymns we have been used to singing in Western churches since the Reformation. But it is perhaps not so different from the Taizé chants, folk-songs and rhythmic choruses from Africa and Asia which are increasingly coming to enliven our worship and broaden our experience of religious music. In music as in art we are perhaps coming much closer than many previous generations to the exuberant abstract imagery of Celtic Christianity with its closeness to nature, its unaffec-ted fervour and its almost dream-like mysticism which seems to blur the dividing line between this world and the next.

As we begin to discard some of the excessive rationalism of Western Christianity we can perhaps begin to appreciate too that other great feature of the Celtic Christian imagin-ation, its tendency to dream dreams and see visions, experi-ence premonitions and feel hidden presences. Such mystical experiences figured prominently in the lives of many of the Celtic saints. St Patrick in his *Confession* recounts eight visions which he saw in dreams, all of which he felt were direct messages from God. The most vivid, and the most important in shaping his life, was that in which he heard what he described as the voice of the Irish coming from a wood near the western sea and saying: 'Holy boy, we are asking you to come and walk among us again'. In one dream he had a sense of a great rock falling on him and pinning him to the ground. He had no doubt that it was the crushing power of Satan. In another he was conscious of someone praying with him: 'I saw him praying in me, and He was as it were within my body and I heard him above me, that is, above the inner man, and there he was praying mightily with groanings'. At first he felt it was Jesus but then he awoke and recalled the text of Romans 8:26: 'the Spirit itself maketh intercession for us with groanings which cannot be uttered'.[6]

Visions while awake were also common. Columba, who is said several times during his life to have seen angels, wrote that 'Heaven has granted to some to see on occasion in their mind, clearly and surely, the whole of earth and sea and sky'. The earliest life of St Fursey, the evangelist of East Anglia, recounts what would nowadays be called a 'near death' experience in which he saw his own soul leaving his body and had a vision of heaven complete with an angelic choir. An eleventh century document graphically describes a more apocalyptic vision experienced by Adamnan involving graphic images of heaven, purgatory and hell.

In part these sightings of angels and visions of the world to come were an aspect of the Celts' great sense of the nearness of God's presence and the thinness of the veil separating this world from the next. They were also, of course, wholly in accordance with scriptural teachings. The Bible is full of dreamers and visionaries from Jacob to the seer of Patmos. The apocalyptic tone of the non-canonical Apocryphal Gospels, which the Celtic Church, like many early Christian communities, seems to have used extensively for reading in public worship, must also have encouraged mystical experiences. But perhaps the most important factor was the Celtic temperament, dreamy and other-worldly, given to possessing second sight and experiencing premonitions and omens. This marked feature of the pagan Celtic outlook was, like so much else, baptised and incorporated into Celtic Christianity. Where pagan Celts had seen fairies and felt premonitions of impending doom, their Christian descendants saw angels and had visions of the Last Judgement.

The extraordinary extent to which Celtic Christians incorporated existing pagan ideas and symbols in their faith is surely the greatest testimony to their powers of imagination.

More clearly than perhaps any other group finding themselves in a missionary situation in a largely pagan land they practised what academics call inculturation, adapting themselves to the prevailing culture and mores of the society in which they lived and preached the Gospel. Most Christian missionaries have been deeply suspicious of the culture of those they have sought to convert and have done all that they can to distance themselves from it. The attitude is well described in that well-known Victorian missionary hymn 'From Greenland's Icy Mountains' which portrays the heathens in their blindness bowing down to wood and stone and crying out for their lands to be delivered from error's chain. As we have seen, the Celtic Christian missionaries had a wholly different attitude towards those with whom they were seeking to share the light of Christ. For them evangelism was more a matter of liberating and releasing the divine spark which was already there in every person than of imposing a new external creed. They did not see the primal pagan religion of the people as a threat to Christianity or a dangerous heresy to be eliminated. Rather it represented, however imperfectly, a stirring of the spiritual and a reaching to the eternal. With imagination and with faith many of its central features and symbols – the standing stones, the sacred groves and springs, the power of circles, the poems, runes and chants – could be baptised and incorporated into Christian worship and witness.

In many ways this approach comes close to what would nowadays be called syncretism. It did not involve a wholesale acceptance of pagan images and practices and a blurring of all distinctions between different religions but it was naturally inclusive and synthetic in spirit, seeking always to incorporate and accommodate different perspectives within the universal embrace of Christ. To a large extent it anticipates the doctrine of 'anonymous Christianity' propounded in the twentieth century by the great Roman Catholic theologian Karl Rahner who argued that Christ dwells, albeit in an unacknowledged and anonymous way, in the hearts of many who would never call themselves Christians. This kind of thinking was not uncommon in the early history of the Church. The great second-century apologist Justin Martyr, for example, argued that the Divine Logos had been in the world from the beginning and that those who lived according to it, whatever their race or declared faith, were truly Christians before the coming of Jesus. Something of the same sense of universality and inclusiveness pervaded Celtic Christianity. With it went the strength of faith and the imagination to see that practices and values associated with other religions could also be part of the great Christian economy of creation and redemption. As the attitude of Christians today towards those of other faiths moves away from notions of confrontation, domination and conversion towards dialogue, listening and mutual sharing and discovery, we can learn much from the approach of our Celtic forefathers.

We could do particularly with developing their sensitive spiritual antennae which were tuned to pick up the religious longings and sentiments that are found in so many people, whether nominally Christian or not. The Celts were a naturally religious people. Even in their so-called pagan state they had experienced a strong sense of divine immanence, felt the sacredness of the earth and believed in an afterlife. Inspired by imagination and faith, their outlook was spiritual rather than materialist. By contrast our modern scientific and secular outlook seeks to find a tidy rational explanation for everything and has no place for angels or presences. For all our intellectual progress and technological developments, the world that we inhabit is in many ways more cramped and confined – black and white where theirs was full of colour, detached and compartmentalised where theirs was holistic and inter-connected. We have lost that outlook which mirrored the central motif of the Celtic knot and where, in the words of Alexander Carmichael, 'religion, pagan or Christian, or both combined, permeated everything – blending and shading into one another like the iridescent colours of the rainbow'.[7]

One of the most striking encapsulations of the difference in outlook between the Celts and contemporary Western Christians was made to me by the late Martin Reith, a priest of the Scottish Episcopal Church who felt called to lead the life of a hermit in the tradition of the Irish anchorites. He characterised it as the contrast between twopence coloured poetry and penny plain prose. His implied criticism of the uninspired dullness of much contemporary religious language will surely strike a chord with all who have despaired at the tortuous quality of much modern theological writing and the flat banality of so many modern prayers. In 1 Corinthians 4:1 St Paul speaks of us as 'stewards of the mysteries of God'. Perhaps one of the most important lessons that we can learn from the Celts' application of imagination to their faith is to turn to the allusive, rhythmical, metaphorical language of poetry when we are seeking to penetrate those mysteries and not attempt to pin them down in the more ponderous, literal, matter-of-fact language of prose.

Preference for expressing ideas and stories in poetry rather than prose runs deep in Celtic culture. It lies behind the whole bardic tradition of chanted lays and epics and the great corpus of incantations, songs and rhymes passed down orally from one generation to another. Poets constituted the intellectual aristocracy of Celtic society, being accorded the kind of status that we now give to media pundits and academics. They were frequently consulted by tribal chiefs, well paid and housed at the public expense. To a considerable extent, as we have seen, Christian monks and scholars took over the role of the old Druidic bards and *filid*. In many ways this was a very natural transition. The Celts regarded poets as having an essentially priestly role in offering up the whole creation to God and standing as intermediaries between this world and the next.

This close affinity between the roles of poet and priest has been underlined in our own time by Donald Allchin. In his book on the Welsh spiritual tradition, *Praise Above All*, he writes:

Both are called, in different ways, to bless; and to bless (*benedicere*) in its original meaning is to speak good things, to declare the goodness which is latent in the world around us, when that world is seen and known as the world of God . . . As poets, all human beings are called to be co-workers with God, co-creators. We are called to discern and proclaim the latent goodness of the creation around us and within us. As priests we are called to offer that goodness back to God in a movement of praise and thanksgiving which is at the same time a movement of intercession and concern.[8]

There is an extensive and distinctive genre in Celtic literature, found particularly but not exclusively in Welsh, which has been categorised as praise poetry. In these poems praise is offered up to God on behalf not just of the human community but the whole of creation. Many of these praise poems are only now being translated from Medieval Welsh by Dr Oliver Davies of University College, North Wales, at Bangor. Their underlying theme, that it is through the medium of poetry that both humans and the whole natural world can come to God, is beautifully expressed in verses penned in English in the seventeenth century by that very Welsh poet whom we remember as the quintessentially English country parson, George Herbert:

> Of all the creatures both in sea and land
> Only to Man thou hast made known thy ways,
> And put the pen alone into his hand,
> And made him secretary of thy praise.
>
> Beasts fain would sing; birds ditty to their notes;
> Trees would be tuning on their native lute
> To thy renown: but all their hands and throats
> Are brought to Man, while they are lame and mute.
>
> Man is the world's High Priest: he doth present
> The sacrifice of all: while they below
> Unto thy service mutter an assent,
> Such as springs use that fall, and winds that blow.[9]

It is significant that a working party set up by the World Council of Churches to draw up a Christian response to the environmental crisis threatening our planet proposed that the role of poet was the most appropriate one for humans to adopt with respect to the rest of creation. Like other artists, poets can depict the variety of creation and affirm its value, distilling its beauty and wonder in ways that touch our imaginations and lead us to God. They can also, perhaps, act as co-creators with God, moving over the face of the waters, fashioning order out of chaos and giving meaning and purpose to existence.

Again and again in Celtic Christianity we find the imagination of the artist and the poet being harnessed, not to explain and pin down the mysteries of the faith or open them up on a dissecting table but to suggest and marvel at their infinite depths and subtleties. This is why there is so much use of images and metaphors from nature, as in the adoption of the wild goose as a symbol of the Holy Spirit and the simple freshness of so many Hebridean prayers:

> As the mist scatters on the crest of the hills,
> May each ill haze clear from my soul, O Lord.[10]

The Roman Church did not have much time for what it regarded as these flights of poetic fancy. It stood for an approach that was more rigorously analytical, more down-to-earth and more prosaic. But even as they were gradually being smothered by the dead hand of Roman imperialism, the Celts hit back with a vigorous defence of the value of the poetic imagination. This Irish poem was written in the mid thirteenth century in reply to a priest who claimed to have come from Rome with a letter condemning the Irish bardic schools.

> To praise man is to praise
> The One who made him,
> And man's earthly possessions
> Add to God's mighty praise.
>
> All metre and mystery
> Touch on the Lord at last,
> The tide thunders ashore
> In praise of the High King.[11]

Too many Christians today, brought up on the penny plain prose favoured by Rome and even more by the Reformers, have half-formed imaginations and react to the twopence coloured poetry of the Celts with a mixture of incomprehension and suspicion. All too often we dismiss the poets and artists in our midst as mere doodlers and dreamers and fail to appreciate that they may be the priests who are interceding for us and articulating our deepest thoughts and concerns to God. We need badly to recover something of the Celtic Christian imagination and its sense of the value of poetry. In the words of Gwendolyn Brooks, 'Poetry is life distilled'. As Saunders Davies says,

The poet has a knack of seeing beneath the surface and is able to find words to express what he sees, what he recognises and what he discerns. Spirit is matter seen from within, matter is spirit seen from without and the poet can make that link. He recognises that life is one whereas today so many people seek to analyse and categorise and divide life into compartments. The poet helps us to see the wholeness of this one God given life, life lived in, through and for the Holy Trinity.[12]

6

The Way Goes On

Although Celtic Christianity was gradually eclipsed in Britain by the more formalised and forbidding creeds of Roman Catholicism and the Protestant Reformation, it has never completely lost its hold on the affections of the people. To some extent going underground and becoming a kind of unofficial folk religion, it survives to this day as a distinctive spiritual tradition particularly in the remoter corners of these islands.

It is in rural Ireland where the distinctive themes of Celtic Christianity still resonate most clearly among a people who have remained remarkably unaffected by the more recent trends of Roman imperialism, Protestant rationalism and secular scepticism. This may well in part be a consequence both of its early escape from foreign invasion and domination at a time when the rest of Britain was subjected to Norman rule and of its more recent political and social isolation. The deeply rooted and idiosyncratic nature of Irish Catholicism has also been a very important factor in preserving aspects of Celtic teaching and spirituality. The landscape of rural Ireland remains demonstrably Celtic, studded with high standing crosses and monasteries, many now sadly reduced to a small handful of elderly monks or closing for lack of vocations. So does the faith of the people, as manifested in the veneration still accorded to St Patrick and the unselfconscious ability to find spiritual significance in the ordinary things of life. Everyday speech still often has a spontaneous religious dimension – the phrase 'thanks be to God' comes tumbling out as a natural coda to many sentences. Among older people particularly there remains a strong sense of the almost physical presence of God and the heavenly host. John Ó'Ríordáin, a Redemptorist priest

100

and passionate enthusiast for Celtic Christianity, told me of an old lady he visited in Drogheda who vehemently protested when he asked her how she managed living alone: 'Oh, I'm never alone. I have Himself always with me and I have Mary and the saints. I am never alone'. As he reflected to me, 'Here she was utterly surrounded with all these people living in the house with her even though a social worker would say here is an old lady living alone. This is living Celtic spirituality'. Another lady whom he visited pointed to a picture of the sacred heart of Jesus on the wall of her kitchen and said to him: 'I'm not speaking to him, Father. We have had a row. I asked him to do something and he didn't do it so now I am just letting him cool his heels a little'.[1]

This sense of an intimate relationship with the Godhead has been a persistent theme of Irish poetry. It is well captured in the poem by Joseph Campbell (1879–1944) which begins:

> I am the gilly of Christ,
>   The mate of Mary's Son;
> I run the roads at seeding time;
>   And when the harvest's done.[2]

Irish literature also reflects other characteristic ideas of Celtic Christianity like the goodness of nature, the value of community and the thin boundary which separates this world and the next. They can be traced in the collection of oral poems and prayers made in the early years of this century by Douglas Hyde, himself a Protestant and the first president of the Irish Republic and the more recent anthology compiled by Patrick Murray and entitled *The Deer's Cry* which surveys Irish religious poetry over the last 2000 years. Recent writers have continued in the tradition. A poem by Patrick Kavanagh, who lived from 1905 to 1967, contains the line 'among your earthiest words the angels stray'. The same sense of the presence of the angels is, of course, found in the sentimental song 'When Irish eyes are smiling' with its line 'in the lilt of Irish laughter you can hear the angels sing'. In rather more literary vein, distinct echoes of Celtic Christianity have recently been traced in the 'subversive spirituality' of James Joyce's *Ulysees* and in the writings of Seán Ó'Ríordáin.[3]

101

It is, as one might expect, among those who still write and speak Irish that the persistence of Celtic Christian influences is most marked. The traditional greeting 'God be with you' is often delivered in Irish in the plural so as to include not just the person being addressed but also the accompanying angelic hosts. Pádraigín Clancy is a scholar of Irish folklore with a particular interest in the traditions of prayer and pilgrimage on the remote Aran Islands off the Galway Bay. She maintains that it is impossible to speak Irish and be an atheist because the language is so suffused by spontaneous religious expressions. In the Aran Islands she finds that the traditional prayers and spirituality of Celtic Christianity are still very much alive: 'There is a sense of the presence of the living spirit all the time. There can be an almost intimate relationship with St Brigid at night when old people on the islands bank down the fire and call on her to help keep it until the morning.'[4]

The survival of these traditional notions of presence and intimacy is now largely confined to the remoter parts of Ireland and to older people who still speak Irish and have not succumbed to the influences of television and creeping Anglicisation and Americanisation. However, Pádraigín Clancy also discerns a real interest in Celtic Christianity among the young:

There's a search on among young people in this country for something beyond the present material myths that are being given in the media. There's a search for what it is to be Irish, something away from just a sense of nationalism, something that is to do with their spirituality and what they're about as Irish people. There's a great interest in exploring the traditions of Celtic Christianity, in the tradition of pilgrimage, for example. Young people are going off on pilgrimage, going to holy wells, doing what their grandparents did without any thought as part of tradition. Young people are almost wanting to find these things back again, to be able to have prayers that relate to everyday life and to bring their spirituality alive. In many ways the current religion which is Roman Catholicism and going to Mass on Sundays hasn't fed and doesn't feed young people adequately. It has failed us as Irish people because we need something that has more tradition to it and that has the sense of God in everything we do – in other words, Celtic spirituality.[5]

Although much of this renewed interest in Celtic themes in Ireland, as elsewhere, is coming from outside the mainstream churches and religious institutions, it is also being actively encouraged by priests within the Roman Catholic Church. Scholars like the Jesuit Diarmud Ó'Laoghaire and the Carmelite Peter O'Dwyer have greatly extended popular knowledge and awareness of the monastic and spiritual traditions of the early Irish Church and have made many ancient prayers and poems widely available to a modern readership. Two younger priests are at the forefront of the movement to revive the values of Celtic Christianity. John Ó'Ríordáin, based in the Redemptorist monastery at Dundalk, emphasises Celtic themes like presence, community and praise in his missionary sermons and is increasingly in demand as a speaker at workshops and conferences on Celtic spirituality in mainland Britain as well as in Ireland. John O'Donoghue, a parish priest in the remote far west of County Galway, adopts a more mystical and philosophical approach, pleading for a recovery of the Celts' sense of the dynamism of the physical world of nature so that 'as we walk through a landscape we may feel not that we are moving through a dead world of inanimate objects but that the landscape we are walking through is alive and that in a very intimate way it is our sister'. To this end, he is working on a Mass of the Ocean and also on a theology of stone, which he regards 'in its silence and in its dignity as the great tabernacle of memory'. Only by recovering the Celtic values of imagination, instinct and identification with nature does he believe that we have any real hope of breaking out of the alienation and exile caused by technology and the modern heresy that everything can be subordinated to the human will.[6]

In Northern Ireland, too, wracked though it is by religious division and hostility, there are signs of an awakening of interest in the gentle and eirenic values of Celtic Christianity. At the forefront of this revival is the ecumenical Corrymeela

Community which is trying so hard to build bridges and break down suspicions between the Roman Catholic and Protestant communities. The Celtic Church was, of course, as firmly rooted in the north of Ireland as in the south – indeed several of its foremost saints, like Columba and Comgall, hailed from what later became Ulster and it was in the city of Armagh that St Patrick established his episcopal see. Maybe the gradual rediscovery of this common Christian heritage, which is neither Roman Catholic nor Protestant and which links the Irish north and the south of the border, may yet help in some small measure towards healing the divisions in this unhappy land.

Scotland also has its religious divisions and a cynic might point out with some justification that the most enduring legacy of the Celtic tradition has been the survival of a football team with a fiercely partisan sectarian following. It is true that 'auld firm' clashes between Celtic and Rangers sometimes show one of the less attractive sides of the Scottish religious tradition. However, it is also true that despite all their perceived dourness and Calvinist severity, it has been Scots Presbyterians who have largely kept the flame of Celtic Christianity burning in the land of Ninian and Kentigern. There are, indeed, echoes of distinctive Celtic practices to be found in the most unlikely places. The Free Church of Scotland which has its stronghold on the Western Isles could hardly be more different in character and theology from the Celtic Church. Yet its practice of singing the psalms unaccompanied in Gaelic with a precentor lining out the notes almost certainly makes the sound and style of its worship closer to that of the early Celtic Christians than any other modern Western Church. Musicologists have recently pointed to close affinities between Gaelic psalm singing and the chanting of the Coptic Churches in North Africa and some have even suggested that this could represent a last surviving example of the strong links which existed between the Churches of the East and the far West in the early Christian centuries.

Much clearer evidence of the enduring legacy of Celtic Christianity can be found immediately south of the Free Church strongholds of Lewis and Harris in the overwhelmingly Catholic islands of South Uist and Barra. It was here a hundred years ago that Alexander Carmichael, himself a Presbyterian, collected most of the Gaelic prayers published in *Carmina Gadelica*. Even today in these largely Gaelic-speaking communities a folk religion survives which owes more to native than to Roman influences and shows distinctive Celtic traits such as a strong sense of presences and premonitions and an acceptance of pagan superstitions and practices. John Angus MacDonald, former parish priest of Daliburgh in South Uist, gave me two examples of such pre-Christian rituals adopted by the Celtic Church which still survive today. When the remains of a deceased person are taken for burial, it is the practice to move round the graveyard in a sunwise or clockwise direction. This habit of moving *diseal* also applies to boats leaving harbour. Another pagan ritual which still survives is the practice of taking a lump of fatty tissue from the breast of a newly killed sheep and hanging it on a rafter of the byre a few days before New Year's Eve. After drying out, it becomes a kind of tallowy candle which is carried round the house and taken three times round the family assembled in the main room as a kind of blessing for the coming year.

The legacy of Celtic spirituality may survive most clearly now among the Gaelic-speaking Catholic communities of the remote Outer Hebrides but it can also be traced in the less obviously receptive soil of mainland Presbyterian Scotland. In his book, *Beyond the Mountains*, Martin Reith identified the prominence of such themes as seeing God through nature in the prayers and poetry of ministers of the Kirk from the seventeenth to the nineteenth century. I have myself identified a strongly Celtic spiritual influence in the devotional meditations and poems of the blind Church of Scotland minister, George Matheson, best known as the author of the hymn, 'O love that wilt not let me go'.[7] The mantle of Pelagius could be said to have fallen on the shoulders of another great Victorian minister, John Macleod Campbell, who was arraigned before the General Assembly of the Church of Scotland in 1831 for preaching the doctrine of universal atonement.

In the twentieth century a trio of distinguished Church of Scotland ministers have in their different ways contributed significantly to the revival of Celtic Christianity. Alistair

Maclean, Gaelic-speaking minister of Daviot in Inverness from 1922 to 1936 and father of the best-selling novelist, published a book of prayers entitled *Hebridean Altars* in 1937. Standing very much within the Celtic tradition, they convey a beautiful and joyful sense of God's presence in all things:

As the hand is made for holding and the eye for seeing,
Thou hast fashioned me for joy.
Share with me the vision that shall find it everywhere:
In the wild violet's beauty;
In the lark's melody;
In the face of a steadfast man;
In a child's smile;
In a mother's love;
In the purity of Jesus.[8]

John Baillie was also a Highlander, born in Gairloch where his father was minister and brought up in Inverness. Appointed professor of theology at Edinburgh University in 1934, he was a man of deep and simple piety and sensitive spirituality. John Macquarrie sees him as heir to the Celtic tradition in his insistence that God is known as presence rather than by inference. Describing God's presence as 'mediated immediacy', Baillie upheld the idea of divine imma-nence at a time when most theologians were stressing trans-cendence and the 'otherness' of God. The theme of pilgrimage also figured prominently in his writings. Perhaps his most influential book, published during the Second World War, was entitled *Invitation to Pilgrimage*.

Undoubtedly the most characteristically and consciously Celtic of leading figures in the Scottish Church in recent times was the man who conceived and accomplished the rebuilding of Iona and established it once again as a great centre of mission. George MacLeod's whole way of life was inspired by the example of the Celtic saints. Long before it became fashionable he was environmentally conscious, running his ancient car on diesel because it caused less pollution than petrol and using batteries powered by windmills to provide the light for his study at Iona. Like the Celts he saw Christ as the centre of the whole created order, the Lord of science and matter as well as of human souls. For him, as for them, the material world was shot through with the spiritual and the whole universe a sacrament. Believing that the atom was as much part of Christ as the human soul, he was wont to change the final verse of the hymn, 'Praise my soul the king of heaven' to 'Atoms help us to adore him, ye behold him face to face'.

George MacLeod's conscious recovery of the great insights of Celtic Christianity led him to stress the themes of intimacy and presence. He spoke unselfconsciously of angels and felt the nearness of the heavenly host and the communion of saints. 'Tell them that we love them and miss them', he would pray about those who had died, 'and long for the day when we shall meet with them again'. He stressed too the importance of finding God in the here and now and in the everyday things of life. As he put it, 'Glory to God in the High Street' was as much a part of the Christian message as 'Glory to God in the highest'. Totally opposed to the dualism and narrow anthropocentrism of contemporary Western Christianity, he preached 'whole salvation' rather than 'soul salvation'. His strong sense of a truly Cosmic Christ present throughout nature was also influenced by Eastern Orthodox theology and scientific theory but it is surely the distinctive note of Celtic spirituality which echoes most clearly through his prayers.

> Invisible we see You, Christ above us,
> With earthly eyes we see above us clouds or sunshine, grey
>   or bright.
> But with the eye of faith we know You reign;
>   instinct in the sun ray,
>   speaking in the storm,
>   warming and moving all Creation, Christ above us.
>
> Invisible we see You, Christ beneath us.
> With earthly eyes we see beneath us stones and dust and
>   dross,
> fit subjects for the analyst's table.
> But with the eye of faith, we know you uphold.
> In You all things consist and hang together:
>   The very atom is light energy,

> The grass is vibrant,
> The rocks pulsate.

All is in flux; turn but a stone and an angel moves.
Underneath are the everlasting arms.
Unknowable we know You, Christ beneath us.[9]

Like Erigena, MacLeod conceived the natural world as dynamic, charged with divine energy, pulsating with life and in a constant state of becoming. Like Pelagius, he had no time for predestination or limited salvation. 'God wills that all people should be saved. Our only problem is whether we are going to accept it, be bathed in it'.[10] On Iona, that 'thin place with only a tissue paper separating earth from heaven',[11] he realised his dream of recreating Columba's missionary community, rebuilding the ruined abbey with the help of unemployed craftsmen and establishing a network of adherents throughout the world bound together by the disciplines of prayer, sharing resources and following a simple lifestyle. Iona is now a place of pilgrimage that attracts upwards of 150,000 people each year. It is also a missionary centre which eschews the hard denominational sell and the crude question 'Are you saved?' in favour of a gentler and more ecumenical approach which works, just as the early Celtic monks did, by building on what is already there rather than by destroying it. As the present leader of the Iona Community, John Harvey, puts it, George Macleod believed 'not so much that the mission was to bring the Gospel to every creature, as that the mission was to bring all mortals to the awareness of the love and purpose of God already present in creation, already breaking through'.[12]

George MacLeod has almost certainly done more than anyone else in the present century to revive Celtic Christianity not as a quaint museum piece or subject for academic study but as a living spiritual force which speaks with a new relevance in our scientifically-minded and environmentally-threatened age. Pilgrim and poet, he tirelessly preached the oneness of creation and the thinness of the line that divides this world and the next. His guiding motif could, indeed, have been the Celtic knot, ever intertwining and interweaving

the sacred and the secular, the material and the spiritual,
endlessly moving, and returning where it started not in a
state of frustration but in a spirit of coming home:

> Follow truth wherever you find it. Even if it takes you
> outside your preconceived ideas of God and life. Even if it
> takes you outside your own country into the most insignifi-
> cant alien places like Bethlehem. Be courageous. But con-
> centrate on your search. Truth is one. All roads lead to
> home.[13]

In Wales, as in Scotland, the Celtic way has taken some
unexpected directions. Indeed, its influence has perhaps been
more clearly felt in the country's periodic Nonconformist
revivals than in Anglican and Roman Catholic church life.
This is partly because of the association of Evangelical Nonconformity with the Welsh language which has been so powerful and expressive a medium for praise and at the same time
a symbol of a marginalised and oppressed people. The rich
corpus of Welsh religious poetry which came out of the Evangelical revival of the eighteenth century is firmly in the tradition of Celtic spirituality. Strongly Trinitarian, it proclaims
the value of community, celebrates the oneness and wonder
of creation and finds God glorified and expressed in nature,
as in this poem written in 1793 by Thomas Jones, a Denbigh
Methodist, about a song-thrush:

> Frail bird of taught loveliness
> You enrich and you astound us.
> We wonder long at your song,
> Your artistry and your voice,
> In you I see, I believe,
> A splendid and unique work of God.[14]

At times highly mystical, as in the lyrics of the Methodist
hymn writer Ann Griffiths, the literature of Welsh revivalism
can also be very down-to-earth, like Howell Harris' prayers
about what kind of stays he should buy for his wife and the
proper dimensions for his bath. The unmistakeable cadences
of Celtic spirituality sound equally through both, as they do

through the great hymn of William Williams Pantycelyn, 'Guide me, O thou great Jehovah', echoing St Patrick's Breastplate in its invocation of the power and strength of God – 'I am weak but thou art mighty' – and powerfully proclaiming the Celtic theme of pilgrimage, As Tudur Jones, the leading contemporary historian of Welsh Nonconformity, has observed,

> It is not surprising if Welsh Evangelical spirituality echoes at many points a very old Christian tradition. Their communal spiritual discipline, as well as their devotion to itinerant preaching and the warmth of their dedication to the service of God, is reminiscent of the enthusiasm of the Celtic saints of long ago who commuted with such energy between Ireland, Scotland, Cornwall, Brittany and Wales.[15]

The distinctive Welsh tradition of praise poetry, mentioned in the last chapter, has its roots in the work of Druidic bards and continues today. It is lovingly and perceptively analysed by Donald Allchin in his recent book, *Praise Above All: Discovering the Welsh Tradition.* He approaches the subject with the eye of an Anglican who is deeply interested in Eastern Orthodoxy and finds many echoes of its spirituality in the predominantly Nonconformist religious poetry of the Welsh. Summing up its overriding theme as the practice of praise, he quotes a definition of its aim by Waldo Williams as being 'to recreate an unblemished world'. Allchin also rejoices in the continuing vitality of the tradition today, noting that 'It is one of the particular joys of meeting with the Welsh-speaking world to find a society in which making poems is still regarded as an ordinary occupation. . . . In the English speaking world unfortunately, the writing of poetry has come to be thought of as special, marginal, extraordinary.'[16]

There is certainly a very strongly spiritual dimension in much modern Welsh poetry and also a very Celtic tendency to find the eternal and the numinous in the everyday things of life. Almost certainly both the best known and the most profound religious poet in Britain in the latter part of the twentieth century has been R. S. Thomas, the Church in Wales priest who now leads a solitary life on the remote Lleyn peninsula in North Wales, which was also the home of many monks and hermits in the heyday of the Celtic Church. Thomas' work is clearly influenced by his Celtic roots. His insistence that matter is 'the scaffolding of the Spirit' recalls the strongly incarnational theology of George Macleod. He is by no means alone among recent and contemporary writers in Welsh in using this kind of religious language. There is a pervasive spirituality and a similar sense of God's presence in the work of many more ostensibly secular poets. A good place to begin a journey of exploration into the spiritual riches of recent Welsh verse is the *Welsh Pilgrim's Manual* edited by Brendan O'Malley, a Scottish Catholic monk turned Church in Wales priest who has done much to revive the practice of pilgrimage in the area around St David's. Here, translated with tremendous sensitivity by Cynthia Saunders Davies, are powerfully affirmative statements of the goodness of God's creation like Donald Evans' 'The Christ of Nature', Alan Llwyd's 'Rebirth', Gwenallt Jones' 'The Creation' and Euros Bowen's 'Gloria' which portrays the very coal under the ground, the bus stops and the railway stations resounding the glory of praise and makes the profound statement that 'to curse life is to err'. Here, too, is Iwan Llwyd's comparison of late 1980s' Cardiff with Bethlehem which ends:

> to the world of the supermarkets
> there came to us also, in the tumult of the night,
> a chance to touch the stars.[17]

My own two particular favourites among modern Welsh poems do not feature in this book although they are contained in a volume entitled *Twentieth Century Welsh Poems* edited and translated by Joseph Clancy and published by Gomer in 1982. Both stand firmly in the Celtic tradition of celebrating the value of community and finding God in the ordinary, every-day things of life. In 'Pigeons' the late Gwenallt Jones recalls the practice in the South Wales' valleys where he was born of the workers keeping pigeons and plays on the fact that in Welsh the same word is used for pigeon and dove. So in his poem the pigeons sent up from the shacks in the back gardens of the grimy mining towns become symbols of the Holy Spirit, 'lumps of beauty in the midst of the haze', sanctifying the smoke and becoming part of the household of God. In 'Having our Tea' Bobi Jones beautifully brings out the sacramentality of one of the simplest and most everyday family activities:

> There's something religious in the way we sit
> At the tea table, a tidy family of three . . .
> Blending calories and words together in the presence
> Of the unseen Conductor who laid the table.[18]

Ireland, Scotland and Wales are the obvious places to look for lingering signs of the survival of a distinctively Celtic spirituality. But its legacy can also be traced in England – and not just in the strange saints' names to be found in Cornish churches and the many dedications to Aidan and Cuthbert in the North East. Some of the greatest English spiritual giants stand in a recognisably Celtic tradition: George Herbert in the seventeenth century with his desire to be taught to see God in all things, echoed two hundred years later by John Keble with his reflection that 'the trivial round, the common task will furnish all I need to ask'; and John and Charles Wesley in the eighteenth century with their stress on sanctification and growth towards perfection, expressed in such phrases as 'changed from glory into glory' and echoing so clearly the theology of Pelagius and Erigena. Maybe in its own subtle and gentle way Lindisfarne has had as much influence as Canterbury on the development of Anglican traditions of spirituality and prayer. I think, for example, of a very Anglican organisation with which I have had the great pleasure of being associated in recent years, the Rural Theology Association. The sensitive, holistic spirituality of its co-founder and first secretary, Mervyn Wilson, whose pilgrim's poem written during a conference on the theme of Creation and the Cross ends this chapter, seems deeply Celtic. Yet he is an almost quintessentially English parish priest whose ministry has been divided between inner city London and rural Northamptonshire.

Robert Van de Weyer, an Anglican priest who is keenly interested in Celtic Christianity, points to a highly visible physical legacy which it has left throughout the British Isles.

In the rest of Europe, he points out, church buildings generally have a rounded wall behind the altar in the style of the ancient Roman basilica. In British churches, by contrast, the east end is almost invariably square in the Celtic style. He also detects a persistent theological legacy, identified by the great Continental theologian Karl Barth when he described British Christianity as 'incurably Pelagian'. Van de Weyer comments: 'The rugged individualism of the Celtic monk, his conviction that each person is free to choose between good and evil, and his insistence that faith must be practical as well as spiritual remain hallmarks of Christians in Britain.' Visitors from other countries, not least the United States, are often shocked at how few people go to church on Sundays. The fact is that, as he points out, 'in Britain the primary test of faith is not religious observance but daily behaviour towards our neighbours and our pets! Indeed, the British love of animals, gardens and nature and our whole tradition of pastoral poetry and landscape painting is another part of our Celtic heritage'.[19]

One might add, in parenthesis, that the influence of Celtic Christianity has not just been confined to the British Isles. Two twentieth century figures who surely came under its spell in their rather different ways were the French biologist and Jesuit priest, Pierre Teilhard de Chardin, and the American monk and writer on contemplative prayer, Thomas Merton. It is perhaps significant that Teilhard hailed from the Auvergne region of France which had been a Celtic stronghold. Like George MacLeod, whom he influenced, he had an intense sense of the sacramentality of the physical universe and of Christ as the Lord of matter as well as spirit, reflected in his description of matter as '*le milieu divin*' and his mass celebrated over the world. For Merton the Celtic spiritual tradition was a more consciously espoused influence rather than something which he grew up with in his blood. Together with the Eastern tradition of the desert fathers it played an important part in leading him towards the eremitical (hermit's) life, enhancing his sense of finding God in nature and opening him to the validity of other religions, notably Hinduism and Buddhism. In his book, *Contemplative Prayer*, he quotes approvingly the poem about the variety of monastic life attributed to St Columba which appeared in Chapter 4.

So the Celtic way continues to inspire pilgrims of many different kinds. But how best can it be followed by Christians today? The answer is at two levels: you can visit the great sites of the Celtic Church and study its surviving artefacts and literary records or you can make the more difficult journey of seeking to follow its practices and values in the often harsh and hostile environment of the modern world.

For the first kind of pilgrimage, which is not without its own great value, the best place to start is Ireland. Here are not only the most enduring and impressive physical monuments of the Celtic Church, the great stone crosses still dotted across the country and the uniquely rich collection of religious works of art gathered together in Dublin but also a popular religious culture which continues to embrace many of the values of the Celtic tradition. An alternative for the armchair traveller who is unable to go to Ireland is to make a literary pilgrimage through the great classics of Celtic spirituality, now mostly available in good modern translations, like St Patrick's *Confession*, Adamnan's *Life of Columba*, the sermons of Columbanus, the *Voyage of Brendan* and the host of early Irish and Welsh poems and prayers. Even more accessible and available in cheaply priced and attractively designed paperbacks are the many recently published selections and translations of the Gaelic prayers and poems collected during the last century by Douglas Hyde in Ireland and Alexander Carmichael in Scotland. It is through these anthologies that many people have been introduced over the last decade or so to Celtic Christianity and they could hardly have had a more appropriate introduction to a faith that was so steeped in both prayer and poetry.

There are, of course, other places to visit on the British mainland which were important Celtic Christian centres and shrines. The trouble is that so often they are now dominated by later buildings, often erected by the Normans and have quite lost their Celtic character. This is true, for example, of Durham and St David's. It is in smaller and remoter places where there is no magnificent medieval cathedral that the atmosphere of the Celtic Church can be more truly experienced. Excavations at Whithorn are revealing something of the shape and nature of the monastery established by St Ninian. The caves and cells associated with Celtic saints which are found along the west coast of Wales and Scotland give some idea of the primitive and solitary lifestyle of the monks and hermits. Most important and evocative of all the Celtic Christian sites in Britain are those two tiny islands, Iona and Lindisfarne, where community life and worship is still being actively pursued in the Celtic tradition. It is here that the two kinds of approach to following the Celtic way merge and intertwine. The visitor who arrives as a tourist becomes a pilgrim and leaves, as Dr Johnson did Iona, spiritually uplifted and changed.

Even on Iona the buildings which help to create the particular atmosphere of spiritual calm and presence are not in fact Celtic. The abbey which has been so lovingly restored is Benedictine, dating from the thirteenth century and witnessing to a very much more formal and enclosed kind of religion than the remains of the simple cells and fragments of high crosses outside which survive from Celtic times. These earlier remains, which it is easy to overlook on a short visit to Iona, take us back to the primitive and provisional structure of the Celtic Church and remind us how close it was to nature and the elements, with its monks living in simple shelters half open to the sky and its worship held outdoors at the foot of the high standing crosses.

What makes Iona so important today, of course, is not its Celtic remains but its work in the field of contemporary Christian mission. It remains first and foremost a place of pilgrimage and attracts seekers of many different kinds but it does not offer them the romantic escapism of a misty Celtic twilight. The community which is based on the abbey preserves a hard cutting edge and a deep involvement in the pains and troubles of the world. This is attested by the fact that its headquarters and the base for much of its activity is situated not on the island but in the heart of inner city Glasgow. People come to stay on Iona to learn more about Celtic spirituality but they come too to share and pray about environmental concerns, commitment to peace and justice, ministering to the marginalised and oppressed and developing inter-faith dialogue. All of these happen to be themes which were also strong in the Celtic Church but that is not the reason why they have been taken up by the Iona Community today. It is almost by coincidence that it finds itself tackling many of the same challenges which faced Columba and his followers 1400 years ago and often adopting similar strategies to meet them. Like them, it finds itself reaching out to many whose beliefs are basically pagan, standing as it does at the interface between conventional Christianity and the New Age movement which has revived aspects of the cultic religion of pre-Christian Britain. Like them too, it has adopted a form of mission which is gentle and unthreatening and which involves getting alongside people, liberating and empowering them and building on what is there rather than seeking to destroy it and impose a new agenda.

One of the Iona Community's most significant contributions to the contemporary Church has undoubtedly been in the area of worship. The community's Wild Goose Group, named after the Celtic symbol for the Holy Spirit, has rejuvenated the worship of countless congregations not just in Scotland but throughout the United Kingdom and abroad. The group's leader, John Bell, is arguably the most innovative and charismatic figure in the field of church worship in contemporary Britain. Much of the inspiration for his liturgies, his dialogues and his fiercely Incarnational hymns and songs has come directly from Celtic Christianity. He singles out three particular influences:

> first, the whole mention of the world as something which is affirmed by God rather than denied; secondly, seeing Jesus as a person, the notion of the Jesus who is MacMary; and thirdly the marriage of the life of the world to the worship of God's people so that you don't have words that you use at work but you never use at church. The Celts managed to overcome that so that whether it was milking the cow or kindling the fire, these were activities in which God could be praised. I've taken that and been very influenced by that in my own writing.[20]

John Bell's songs, which are often set to traditional Scottish folk tunes, like 'Dance and Sing', 'A Touching Place' and 'Will you come and follow me', are among the most significant contemporary expressions of Celtic Christianity. So are the liturgies produced by the Wild Goose Group, many of which use adaptations of traditional Gaelic prayers. I know of no liturgical group in any church which is doing more to make modern worship less conceptual and wordy and to introduce the kind of imagery favoured in both the Celtic and Eastern Orthodox traditions. I recall taking part in a worship workshop led by John Bell and his Iona colleague Graham Maule in which we were thrown a pile of old magazines and colour supplements and asked to cut out pictures which in some way represented our idea of God. The pictures were then put together on the ground and candles lit around them. In the whole act of worship there was very little speaking and yet its effect was profound and very memorable.

Lindisfarne has also and more recently become a place where the particular power of Celtic liturgy is being rediscovered and interpreted for our own age. The inspiration has come almost entirely from David Adam, who has since 1990 been the vicar of Holy Island. His anthologies of old and new prayers in the Celtic tradition, *The Edge of Glory* and *Tides and Seasons* have rightly become best-sellers. Their simplicity, directness and sensitivity appeal to people of widely different denominational backgrounds and religious persuasions. I myself have found them particularly helpful in pastoral work with those suffering from mental illness, especially schizophrenia and depression. Like the Celts, they often feel an almost physical sense of evil and possession and are greatly helped by the prayers of encirclement and protection which have largely dropped out of modern liturgies.

David Adam is currently trying to strengthen Lindisfarne as a centre for retreats and conferences. It may even be that like Iona it will come to house a religious community, based not on the rigidly structured and enclosed pattern of the medieval monastery but the looser and more open Celtic model. There are other residential religious communities in England which have been set up in recent years where Celtic monastic life has been an important inspiration. The most notable example is perhaps the Little Gidding Community in

Cambridgeshire established in 1977 by Robert Van de Weyer and his wife, Sarah, which continues to flourish with around thirty members pursuing their own jobs but meeting regularly for communal worship and meals. Van de Weyer strongly believes that it is in such *ad hoc* communities rather than in the more traditional institutions with their heavy dependence on expensive buildings, ordained clergy and cumbersome bureaucracy that the future of the church may lie.

The Celtic Church, as we have seen, was not a highly organised and hierarchical institution but rather a loose grouping of local communities of prayer, learning and hospitality. Like the base Christian communities of Latin America and the churches of Africa and Asia, its keynotes were spontaneity and provisionality. Its members met for worship not in great cathedrals and solid stone churches but at the foot of high crosses, in forest glades and clearings or in simple wattle and daub huts. They were a pilgrim people, ever on the move and always looking ahead. It may well be that this is the way forward now for Christians in the so-called developed world and that the third millenium will see a return to those localised and provisional communities which flourished in the first one, leaving the highly structured institutions and elaborate church buildings with which we have been familiar for the last thousand years looking increasingly like ecclesiastical dinosaurs.

This is not to say that we need a new philistinism and iconoclasm that would happily let beautiful old churches fall into ruins, choirs disband and ancient liturgies disappear. This would not be to follow the Celtic way at all. Celtic Christianity did not destroy cultural traditions and roots – it built on them and baptised them. It may have had a strongly ascetic and even austere quality but it was not puritanical or narrow in its sympathies. Indeed, it enthusiastically embraced music, art and poetry. The Celtic monasteries were not just mission stations – they were centres of culture and enlightenment, little colonies of heaven which witnessed not just to the narrow Gospel of individual redemption but to Jesus' wider promise of life in all its fulness. As Europe entered the Dark Ages they kept alight not just the Christian flame but the beacon of art, culture and learning.

It is not, I think, being unduly pessimistic to suggest that we are entering another Dark Age. The threat now comes not from savage tribes like the Vandals, Goths and Huns but from the brutalising pressures of advertising and the mass media, the crudeness and violence of much popular music and entertainment and the inexorable rise of the consumer society with its rampant acquisitiveness and selfishness. If the churches are to make any kind of effective stand for the Christian values which are increasingly under attack it is surely by following the example of the Celtic monasteries and becoming little pools of gentleness and enlightenment, oases of compassion and charity in the ever extending desert of secular materialism. This will not be an easy calling. It will mean modern Christians becoming like the Celtic monks and pilgrims, never feeling quite at home or at rest in this world, ever seeking their place of resurrection and constantly invoking God's presence and protection against evil forces. But we will also have much to help us on our way: the inspiration of music, art and poetry, the refreshment of nature, and the companionship not just of fellow pilgrims among the living but also of the whole host of heaven, that great company who have already travelled the way before us.

Ministers are notorious for alliteration and for dividing their sermons into three points. I fear I am going to succumb to both temptations as I come to the conclusion of this book. Three 'p's could be taken as the distinguishing hallmarks of Celtic Christianity – presence, poetry and pilgrimage. They have all been rather neglected by the churches of the Western world over the last thousand years. I would like to argue strongly for their recovery.

We are at last beginning to turn our backs on centuries of subscribing to dualist ideas and over-stressing divine transcendence and coming to recognise God's animating presence where we have previously denied or overlooked it – in the world of nature, in the everyday things of life, in the atoms and molecules that are the basic constituents of all matter. We still have a long way to go, however, in recovering the Celts' wonderful and all-embracing sense of every part of the world and every aspect of life being filled with the presence of God. If we do recover it in time, perhaps we will yet save the planet that we have so nearly destroyed. Presence is important in another rather different sense as well. The kind of ministry undertaken by the Celtic Church could perhaps best be described as a ministry of presence. Its monasteries were presences in society which witnessed to the Gospel as much just by being there as by activity and involvement in schemes and projects. There is great stress now in many churches on always doing things, being constantly active, launching new projects and setting new targets. Certainly the church should always be on the move and never standing still, but there is something to be said for encouraging the doodlers and dreamers as well as the doers and planners. We could do with more bards and poets in the modern church and, dare one say, with fewer committees and task forces.

I often reflect on Martin Reith's distinction between the twopence coloured poetry of the Celts and the Anglo-Saxon preference for penny plain prose that has come to predominate in the language and liturgy of our churches. Both theology and worship have become too prosy, over-intellectual and often dull and leaden as a result. We need to learn from the Celts to express our faith in images rather than concepts. In a culture dominated by television and visual imagery this is particularly important. We need to find and develop our own evangelistic aids with the power of the high standing crosses to stop people in their tracks and contemporary icons which will encourage meditation and contemplation as the illuminated manuscripts once did. We need too to recover more widely that rich Christian poetic imagination which still exists in Wales and to stop trying to tie down the ineffable mystery and beauty of God in mere prose.

The third and final 'p' that we would do well to recover from our Celtic Christian ancestors takes us back to those endlessly intertwining ribbons and ever curling spirals of which they were so fond. At the root of the Celts' attachment to the idea of pilgrimage was their understanding that nothing is static. Long before anyone was talking about relativity, quantum mechanics or process thought, they appreciated the essentially open-ended and dynamic character of the universe and realised that creation is a continuous process rather than a once-and-for-all activity in the dim and distant past. They saw, too, that human life is also in a constant state of development, change and growth, charged like the rest of creation with the potentialising energy of Christ, ever becoming rather than just being. To be a pilgrim was to take the outward path which acknowledged the reality of this inner journey of the individual human soul and to embark on a way which involved suffering, sacrifice and pain as well as consolations and companionship along the way and which ended, if indeed it ended at all, at the place of one's resurrection.

We too can both lose and find ourselves as pilgrims within the twists and turns of the Celtic knot, that elusive symbol with which I began this journey along the Celtic way. If it seems a mass of detours and diversions, false trails and cul de sacs, then that is the way that the Lord marked out for his pilgrim people Israel when he led them out of Egypt not on the most direct track but by a roundabout route. If it offers endless opportunities along the way, it is also the path of waiting and suffering, disappointments and frustrations, the *via dolorosa* which leads to the Cross. In the end it brings us back to where we began, to the one who is the Alpha and Omega, the beginning and the end of our journey. The Celtic knot interweaves the old and the new, the pagan and the Christian, the sacred and the secular, nature and grace, creation and redemption, matter and spirit, masculine and feminine, this world and the next. Along its tangled and twisting threads, with their reminder that all is connected and nothing stands alone, we can make our own journeys of faith and experience, with all their risks and possibilities, circumscribed only by the constant guidance and protection of God who ever enfolds and encircles us.

> You who would travel the highway of faith
> Do not look back, do not stay,
> You who have grasped the great circle
> Trust God, the world will own his day.
>
> Do not try to recapture, but do not devalue
> The vintage once you knew.
> The gospel ever explodes yesterday's vessel,
> The wine comes fresh for you.

Two meet, three meet at a turn of the road
Travelling with the one Lord.
Each must move on within the same circle
True together to his word.

You who would travel God's great highway
Unmapped, ahead, heaven's way,
With the one, with many never at rest,
Do not look back nor stay.[21]

Notes

CHAPTER 1   A PROCESSION OF SAINTS AND SCHOLARS

1. H. Richardson, 'Observations on Christian Art in Early Ireland, Georgia and Armenia' in M. Ryan (ed.), *Ireland and Insular Art, AD 500–1200* (Royal Irish Academy, Dublin, 1987), p. 130.
2. T. Ó Fiaich, 'Irish Monks on the Continent' in J. Mackey (ed.), *An Introduction to Celtic Christianity*, (T. and T. Clark, Edinburgh, 1989), pp. 101–35.
3. S. Toulson, *The Celtic Alternative* (Century Hutchinson, London, 1987), pp. 10–11.

CHAPTER 2   PRESENCE AND PROTECTION

1. The full text can be found in J. Mackey (ed.), *An Introduction to Celtic Christianity*, pp. 47–8.
2. J. Macquarrie, *Paths in Spirituality* (SCM Press, London, 1972), pp. 22–3.
3. P. Murray (ed.), *The Deer's Cry. A Treasury of Irish Religious Verse* (Four Courts Press, Dublin, 1986), p. 15.
4. A. Carmichael, *Carmina Gadelica* (5 vols., Oliver and Boyd, Edinburgh, 1928–54), III, 307.
5. S. Davies, 'Light in Darkness – the Relevance of Celtic Spirituality Today' (unpublished paper, quoted with permission), p. 15.
6. *Carmina Gadelica*, II, 274–5.
7. H. J. Massingham, *The Tree of Life* (Chapman and Hall, London, 1943), p. 37.
8. *Carmina Gadelica*, I, xxxiii.
9. Interview with author for BBC Seeds of Faith programme.

10. J. Mackey (ed.), *op. cit.*, p. 12.
11. J. Macquarrie, *op. cit.*, p. 123.
12. *Carmina Gadelica*, I, 231.
13. *Ibid.*, I, 233.
14. *Ibid.*, I, 331.
15. Quoted in E. De Waal, *The World Made Whole: Rediscovering the Celtic Tradition* (Fount, 1991), p. 76.
16. S. Davies, *loc. cit.*, p. 9.
17. *Carmina Gadelica*, III, 333.
18. *Adamnan's Life of Columba*, edited and translated by A. O. and M. O. Anderson (Clarendon Press, Oxford, 1991), p. 191.
19. A. Maclean, *Hebridean Altars* (Moray Press, Edinburgh, 1937), p. 142.
20. D. Adam, *Tides and Seasons* (Triangle/SPCK, London, 1989), p. 105.
21. N. O' Donoghue, 'St Patrick's Breastplate' in J. Mackey (ed.), *op. cit.*, pp. 45–63.
22. *Carmina Gadelica*, I, 231.

CHAPTER 3   THE GOODNESS OF NATURE

1. G. Murphy (ed.), *Early Irish Lyrics* (Clarendon Press, Oxford, 1956), p. 5.
2. A. M. Allchin, *Praise Above All: Discovering the Welsh Tradition* (University of Wales Press, Cardiff, 1991), p. 11.
3. K. Meyer (ed.), *Selections from Ancient Irish Poetry* (Constable, London, 1911), p. 30.
4. *Adamnan's Life of Columba*, p. 87.
5. *Ibid.*, p. 223.
6. Translation by Brendan Kennelly.
7. K. Meyer (ed.), *op. cit.*, xii.
8. *Carmina Gadelica*, I, 39–41.
9. Quoted in D. Adam, *Tides and Seasons*, p. 33.
10. John the Scot, *Periphyseon: the Division of Nature* translated by M. L. Uhlfelder (Bobbs-Merrill Company, Indianapolis, 1976), ix.
11. J. J. O'Meara, *Eurigena* (Clarendon Press, Oxford, 1988), p. 112.
12. Quoted in T. Finan, 'Hiberno-Latin Christian Literature' in J. Mackey (ed.), *An Introduction to Celtic Christianity*, p. 80.
13. H. J. Massingham, *The Tree of Life*, p. 40.

14. N. O'Donoghue, *Patrick of Ireland* (Michael Glazier, Wilmington, Delaware, 1987), p. 93.

CHAPTER 4 MONKS AND PILGRIMS

1. E. Hull (ed.), *The Poem Book of the Gael* (Chatto and Windus, London, 1912), p. 112.
2. I am indebted to Fr Peter O'Dwyer for these quotations.
3. *Bede's Ecclesiastical History of the English People*, edited by B. Colgrave and R. A. B. Mynors (Clarendon Press, Oxford, 1969), p. 313.
4. D. Adam, *The Cry of the Deer* (Triangle/SPCK, London, 1987), p. 28.
5. Interview with author for BBC Radio programme.
6. J. J. Ó'Ríordáin, *Irish Catholics: Tradition and Transition* (Veritas, Dublin, 1980), pp. 24–5.
7. G. Murphy (ed.), *Early Irish Lyrics*, p. 19.
8. *The Age of Bede* translated by J. F. Webb (Penguin, London, 1965), p. 245.
9. J. J. Ó'Ríordáin, *op. cit.*, p. 25.
10. *Sancti Columbani Opera* edited by G. S. M. Walker (Dublin Institute for Advanced Studies, 1957), pp. 95–7.
11. Quoted in T. Finan, 'Hiberno-Latin Christian Literature' in J. Mackey (ed.), *An Introduction to Celtic Christianity*, p. 73.
12. T. S. Eliot, *The Four Quartets*, 'Little Gidding' (Faber).

CHAPTER 5 THE POWER OF IMAGINATION

1. E. Hull (ed.), *The Poem Book of the Gael*, p. 237.
2. Interview with author for BBC radio programme.
3. Interview with author for BBC radio programme.
4. N. O'Donoghue, 'The presence of God in the *Carmina Gadelica*' (unpublished paper, quoted with permission), p. 8.
5. *Carmina Gadelica*, I, pp. 2–3.
6. Patrick's dreams and visions are described and analysed in N. O'Donoghue, *Patrick of Ireland* to which I owe these references.
7. *Carmina Gadelica*, I, xxxiii.
8. A. M. Allchin, *Praise Above All*, pp. 6, 8.
9. 'Providence'. The text of the complete poem can be found in G. Herbert, *The Complete English Poems* (Penguin, 1991), pp. 108–13.
10. *Carmina Gadelica*, III, p. 31.

11. A. M. Allchin, *op. cit.*, p. 9.
12. Interview with author for BBC radio programme.

CHAPTER 6   THE WAY GOES ON

1. Interview with author for BBC radio programme.
2. L. Robinson (ed.), *A Golden Treasury of Irish Verse* (Macmillan, London, 1925), p. 222.
3. J. S. O'Leary, 'The Spiritual Upshot of *Ulysees*' and R. Welch, 'Seán Ó'Ríordáin: An Existential Tradition' in J. P. Mackey (ed.), *An Introduction to Celtic Christianity*.
4. Interview with author for BBC radio programme.
5. *Ibid.*
6. *Ibid.*
7. I. C. Bradley (ed.), *O Love that Wilt Not Let me Go: Meditations, Prayers and Poems by George Matheson* (Fount, 1990).
8. A. Maclean, *Hebridean Altars*, p. 125.
9. G. Macleod, 'Man is Made to Rise' in *The Whole Earth Shall Cry Glory* (Wild Goose Publications/Iona Community, Glasgow, 1985). Reproduced by permission.
10. Sermon, 'Modern Man and Prayer', July 1955, quoted in *Daily Readings with George Macleod*, ed. R. Ferguson (Fount, 1990), p. 144.
12. Interview with author for BBC radio programme.
13. Advent talk, December 1955, quoted in *Daily Readings*, p. 75.
14. Quoted in A. M. Allchin, *Praise Above All*, p. 32.
15. R. T. Jones, 'The Evangelical Revival in Wales: A Study in Spirituality' in J. P. Mackey, *op. cit.*, p. 267.
16. A. M. Allchin, *op. cit.*, p. 8.
17. B. O'Malley (ed.), *A Welsh Pilgrim's Manual* (Gomer, Llandysul, 1989), p. 106.
18. B. Jones, *Selected Poems* translated by J. Clancy (Christopher Davies, Swansea, 1987), p. 63.
19. Interview with author for BBC radio programme. See also R. Van de Weyer, *Celtic Fire* (Darton, Longman and Todd, London, 1990).
20. Interview with author for BBC radio programme.
21. Poem by Mervyn Wilson written during 1991 Rural Theology Conference on 'Creation and the Cross'. Reproduced by permission.

Suggestions
for Further Reading

Celtic Christianity is very much a 'live' area of historical, archaeological, literary and theological study and new books are coming out every year with fresh discoveries and perspectives. The list below is by no means exhaustive and is designed simply to point the reader to some of the recent works that I have found particularly helpful as well as to some older books which still have much valuable information, even if they have been superseded or challenged on certain points. The place of publication is London except where otherwise stated.

GENERAL WORKS ON THE CELTS AND CELTIC BRITAIN

Charles Thomas, *Celtic Britain* (Thames and Hudson, 1986).
Nora Chadwick, *The Celts* (Penguin, 1971 and frequent reprints).
Barry Cunliffe, *The Celtic World* (Bodley Head, 1979).
Miranda Green, *Symbol and Image in Celtic Religious Art* (Routledge, 1989).
Caitlin Matthews, *The Celtic Tradition* (Element Books, Shaftesbury, 1989).

HISTORIES OF THE CELTIC CHURCH

Charles Thomas, *Christianity in Roman Britain* (Batsford, 1981).
Louis Gougaud, *Christianity in Celtic Lands* (Sheed and Ward, 1932).
L. Hardinge, *The Celtic Church in Britain* (SPCK, 1972).
Douglas Simpson, *The Celtic Church in Scotland* (Aberdeen University Press, 1935).

Andrew Patterson, *Whithorn, Iona and Lindisfarne: A Celtic Saga* (St Andrew's Press, Edinburgh, 1991).
John Walsh and Thomas Bradley, *A History of the Irish Church, 400–700* AD (Columba Press, Blackrock, Dublin, 1991).

BIOGRAPHIES AND STUDIES OF CELTIC SAINTS AND THEOLOGIANS

Noel O'Donoghue, *Aristocracy of Soul: Patrick of Ireland* (Wilmington, Delaware, 1987).
Richard Hanson, *Saint Patrick: His Origins and Career* (Oxford, 1968).
Douglas Simpson, *The Historical Saint Columba* (Aberdeen, 1927).
Ian Finlay, *Columba* (London, 1967).
B. R. Rees, *Pelagius: A Reluctant Hero* (Boydell Press, Woodbridge, 1988).
J. J. O'Meara, *Eurigena* (Clarendon Press, Oxford, 1988).
H. Bett, *Johannes Scotus Erigena* (Russell and Russell, New York, 1964).
John the Scot, *Periphyseon: the Division of Nature* translated by M. L. Uhlfelder (Bobbs-Merrill Company, Indianapolis, 1976).
Edwin Sprott Towill, *The Saints of Scotland* (St Andrew Press, Edinburgh, 1983).
The Penguin Dictionary of Saints (Penguin, 1983).

BOOKS TRACING THE MAIN THEMES AND CONTINUING LEGACY OF CELTIC CHRISTIANITY

Martin Reith, *Beyond the Mountains* (SPCK, 1979).
Shirley Toulson, *The Celtic Alternative* (Century Hutchinson, 1987).
Esther de Waal, *The World Made Whole* (Fount, 1991).
James Mackey (ed.), *An Introduction to Celtic Christianity* (T and T Clark, Edinburgh, 1989).
John J. Ó'Ríordáin, *Irish Catholics – Tradition and Transition* (Veritas, Dublin, 1980).
Michael Maher (ed.), *Irish Spirituality* (Veritas, Dublin, 1981).
A. M. Allchin, *Praise Above All. Discovering the Welsh Tradition* (University of Wales Press, Cardiff, 1991).
David Adam, *The Cry of the Deer – Meditations on the Hymn of St Patrick* (Triangle/SPCK, 1987).

STUDIES ON CELTIC CHRISTIAN ART

Françoise Henry, *Early Christian Irish Art* (Dublin, 1954).

Hilary Richardson and John Scarry, *An Introduction to Irish High Crosses* (Mercier Press, Cork, 1990).

G. O. Simms, *Irish Illuminated Manuscripts* (Eason, Dublin, 1985).

J. Romilly Allen, *Celtic Crosses of Wales* (Llanerch Publishers, Felinfach, 1989).

Derek Bryce, *Symbolism of the Celtic Cross* (Llanerch Enterprises, Felinfach, 1989).

ANTHOLOGIES OF CELTIC PRAYERS AND POEMS

Alexander Carmichael, *Carmina Gadelica* (5 vols., Oliver and Boyd, Edinburgh, 1928–54).

Alexander Carmichael, *The Sun Dances, Prayers and Blessings from the Gaelic* (Floris Books, Edinburgh, 1988).

Alexander Carmichael, *New Moon of the Seasons, Prayers and Blessings from the Gaelic* (Floris Books, Edinburgh, 1988).

Esther de Waal, *The Celtic Vision – Prayers and Blessings from the Outer Hebrides* (Darton, Longman and Todd, 1988).

Esther de Waal and A. M. Allchin, *Threshold of Light – Prayers and Praises from the Celtic Tradition* (Darton, Longman and Todd, 1988).

Robert Van de Weyer, *Celtic Fire – An Anthology of Celtic Christian Literature* (Darton, Longman and Todd, 1990).

G. R. D. McLean, *Praying with Highland Christians* (Triangle/SPCK, 1988).

David Adam, *The Edge of Glory – Prayers in the Celtic Tradition* (Triangle/SPCK, 1985).

David Adam, *Tides and Seasons – Modern Prayers in the Celtic Tradition* (Triangle/SPCK, 1989).

Brendan O'Malley, *A Welsh Pilgrim's Manual* (Gwasg Gomer, Llandysul, 1989).

Christopher Bamford and William Parker Marsh, *Ecology and Holiness: The Heritage of Celtic Christianity* (Floris Books, Edinburgh, 1986).

Martin Reith, *God in our midst: Prayers and devotions from the Celtic tradition* (Triangle/SPCK, 1989).

Patrick Murray (ed.), *The Deer's Cry. A Treasury of Irish Religious Verse* (Four Courts Press, Blackrock, Dublin, 1986).

Eleanor Hull (ed.), *The Poem Book of the Gael* (Chatto and Windus, 1912).

Kuno Meyer (ed.), *Selections from Ancient Irish Poetry* (Constable, 1911).

Gerard Murphy (ed.), *Early Irish Lyrics* (Clarendon Press, Oxford, 1956).

Index of
Names and Places

Aaron, St, 5
Adam, David, x, 47, 49, 75, 117
Adamnan, St, 45, 56, 91, 93, 114
Agricola, Roman soldier, 5
Aidan, St, 21
Alban, St, 5
Aldhelm, St, 22
Alexander, Mrs C. F., 31
Alfred, King, 80
Allchin, Donald, x, 85, 96, 110
Amergin, prince of Ireland, 34
Anglesey, 12
Annegray (France), 16
Anselm, St, 66
Antony, St, 9, 10, 78
Ardagh (Ireland), 28, 89
Arles (France), 22
Armagh (Northern Ireland), 13,
    27, 29, 71, 104
Assisi (Italy), 56
Athanasius, St, 9
Athelstan, Saxon king, 26
Augustine of Canterbury, St, 22
Augustine of Hippo, St, 51, 52,
    62–3, 66, 69

Baillie, John, 106
Bangor (Northern Ireland), 14, 16,
    17
Bangor (North Wales), 18, 29
Bardsey Island (North Wales), 78
Barth, Karl, 113
Bede, 11, 55, 74
Bell, John, ix, 116–17

Birdoswald (Cumbria), 12
Bobbio (Italy), 17, 56
Bosham (Sussex), 22
Bowen, Euros, 111
Bradwell-on-Sea (Essex), 21
Bran, pagan voyager, 79
Brechin Scotland), 4
Bregenz (Austria), 16
Brendan, St, 12, 14, 40, 79
Bridget, pagan goddess, 5, 15
Brigid, St, 14, 15, 40, 73, 102
Brooks, Gwendolyn, 99
Brude, king of the Picts, 20
Buite, St, 14

Caerleon (South Wales), 5
Caerwent (South Wales), 12
Caldey Island (South Wales), 18
Callanish (Lewis), 86
Campbell, John Macleod, 105
Campbell, Joseph, 101
Canmore, Michael, 27
Canterbury, 22, 25, 26, 112
Carmichael, Alexander, 34, 35, 37,
    39, 49, 91, 92, 95, 105, 114
Carter, Sydney, 82
Carthach, St, 14
Cathald, St, 17
Cedd, St, 21
Celestine I, Pope, 12
Chad, St, 21
Ciaran, St, 14, 55
Clancy, Joseph, 111
Clancy, Pádraigín, ix, 102

131